The Rod Stewart Companion

The Rod Stewart Companion

Edward Wincentsen

Wynn Publishing

WYNN PUBLISHING
P.O. Box 1491
Pickens, SC 29671

864-878-6469
wynnpub@wynnco.com

First Printing, October, 2000

Copyright 2000 Wynn Publishing

Library of Congress
Control Number: 00-134532

ISBN: 0-9642808-5-X

All rights reserved. No part of this work may be reproduced or transmitted in whole or part in any form without written permission of the publisher. Brief quotations may be used for the purpose of reviews.

This book is not endorsed or authorized by Rod Stewart, or his representatives.

Book design & layout: Edward Wincentsen
Printed in the USA

Dedicated to
all the fans
around the world

Rod Stewart
A Biographical Profile

When Rod Stewart was born the world had no idea that a rocker had come on the scene. But Rod the Mod would soon prove to the world that he had what it takes to dish out the music in his own individual style. And his music did capture the attention of the world! Rod has been known as a 'accessible, touchable' star. He enjoys pleasing the fans in concert and is not afraid to mingle with them in between concerts. He calls the fervent fans 'tartan hordes.'

In school, at William Grimshaw, Rod was classmates with Ray and Dave Davies, later The Kinks. School did not hold much interest to Rod and he was very often not there or forgetting his homework. The entertainer/singer Al Jolson was a big influence on Stewart in his early years and Rod wanted to be like him. Finally, Rod would leave school at the age of fifteen with no educational certificates to show for his time there.

In later years, Rod's rabid devotion to Scotland, his father's birthplace, was the basis on which he would consider himself a Scot. The freewheeling world of the beatnik attracted Rod. Roaming free was Rod's ambition as a seventeen-year-old. Something inside of Rod's head must have been leading him to the life of an artist. This trait in Rod at an early age surely must serve him to this day as he travels the road as the gypsy entertainer. Rod said, "I had no ambition at the time, but to be famous....I just had to be famous."

During one of his times living with his parents he worked three weeks as a grave digger. He admitted to his fear of death and said that he believed the only way to tackle that kind of fear was to face up to it. "That's why I dug graves for awhile."

Rod's next change after his beatnik days was to latch on to the Mod look and fashion of Swinging London. As for music he always preferred the raw, authentic sound of The Rolling Stones to that of the Beatles. The story that is often told is about how Rod Steward was discovered by Long John Baldry. The place was the Twickenham railway station on the night of Sunday, January 7, 1964. Rod had been at the Eel Pie Island club to see Baldry and his band. Baldry heard Stewart playing 'Smokestack Lighting' on his harmonica. Baldry asked him to join his band, Rod asked how much pay there was and accepted the job there on the spot.

John Rowlands and producer, Mike Vernon saw Rod Stewart singing with Long John Baldry and His Hoochie Men and felt that Rod had talent that could surpass his present band. They signed Rod to a management contract. Shortly after that Mike Vernon got Rod a solo recording contract with Decca Records.

Rod Stewart made his television debut singing the song 'Good Morning Little Schoolgirl' on the popular show Ready, Steady, Go. It was at a pup after the program that Rod first met guitarist Ronnie Wood.

In the pop world of England of the 1960's Giorgio

Gomelsky was a well known figure. From his club, The Crawdaddy, came some of the most important bands of the era. His influence reached from the early days of The Rolling Stones to the heady days of Swinging London. Gomelsky managed keyboard man, Brian Auger who's own band, Trinity, was already very popular. Gomelsky talked the Yardbirds secretary, Julie Driscoll, into going and seeing the Trinity as he announced that she would be singing with the band along with Rod Stewart and Long John Baldry. He was naming the group Steam Packet. Besides Rod, Baldry, Auger and Driscoll, Gomelsky was adding Rick Brown on bass, Vic Briggs on guitar (later with Eric Burdon's second Animals) and drummer Mickey Waller.

Steam Packet was short lived mainly because no one wrote any original material. Their biggest gig was playing two shows on the same bill as The Rolling Stones August 1, 1964 at the London Palladium. Rod left Steam Packet in the spring of 1966 after being fired by Brian Auger. Just a few months later the band itself folded.

Rik and John Gunnell, who owned a London club, came up with the idea of a new supergroup to be comprised of Rod, Liverpool-born singer Beryl Marsden, keyboardist Peter Bardens, Dave Ambrose on bass and genius guitarist Peter Green along with expert drummer Mick Fleetwood (the two who later formed the foundation of the very successful Fleetwood Mac). The band lasted for seven months, calling it over at the end of 1966.

Andrew Oldham, the manager of The Rolling Stones, had a new record label called Immediate Records. Mick Jagger at this time was interested in producing. Andrew and his partner, Tony Calder wanted Rod Stewart on the new label when they

Rare, early photo of Rod with Eric Burdon and Long John Baldry.

found out that Rod was now without a record label. Calder said that both Andrew and himself wanted Rod, but that Mick Jagger was very jealous.

Rod joined the Jeff Beck Group along with bandmate Ronnie Wood, but Beck and Stewart were like oil and water. Problems started when Beck fired Ronnie Wood and drummer Mickey Waller. Rod finally quit the band in July 1969. Rod stated that during his time with the Jeff Beck Group was when his voice started to change. He was twenty-four. Ronnie Wood joined the London group The Small Faces and he told Rod that the group needed a new singer as well.

A recording contract with Warner Brothers was secured for The Small Faces by a Billy Gaff. The Small Faces had the reputation of being a hard drinking band. At this same time Rod had a solo recording contract with Mercury Records. Mercury allowed Rod to record his solo, debut album with the Small Faces as his backing band. The album was released in February of 1970 and was called 'The Rod Stewart Album' in America.

Rod's enthusiasm for money was always remarked on by his friends and colleagues. In Ray Coleman's biography he stated that Rod has always hated being lied to. "He always wants the bottom line, even if that brings bad news. If you deceive him just once, there is no room for you in his life anymore."

Rod always rated Mickey Waller's work as a drummer as exceptional and kept him for his studio work. 'Gasoline Alley' was Rod's second solo album. Rod's third solo album was 'Every Picture Tells A Story' and it was a smash hit! Rod had finally come into his element as a strong songwriter. Rod's song 'Maggie May' launched his career as well as helping to sell the new album. October 9, 1971 found Rod's album and single at number 1 in the charts, both in the USA and in England. Rod became a millionaire!

During the success of Rod's solo work he continued on with the band Small Faces. Their album 'A Nod's as Good as a Wink to a Blind Horse' went to number 2 in the British charts and 17 in the American charts.

Rod's first serious romance was with Dee Harrington. She was twenty-one when Rod met her, daughter of a RAF squadron leader. Dee had been in Los Angeles for four months on holiday when her friends took her to a Faces promotional party July 29, 1971 where she met Rod. The following evening she attended a Faces concert for the first time at the Long Beach Arena. Soon Dee moved into Rod's new Broad Walk, Winchmore Hill, North London mock Tudor house. Their relationship lasted for four years.

In 1972 Rod's fourth solo album 'Never A Dull Moment' was released. It went to the top in America.

Rod has stated that he hates songwriting and the recording process. The only aspect of his career that he really enjoys is the performing. "If I couldn't perform I'd give it up. The only thing I get a buzz from is getting up and playing. When that goes, I'll go with it. Do like the pro-footballers, retire at the top."

Rod's days with the Faces was starting to come to an end. In an interview with Roy Hollingworth for Melody Maker Rod lashed out with his feelings about Faces and their last album together. After an American tour Faces returned to Britain and band member Ronnie Lane quit the group. Rod then went to the group Free and got their bass player, Japanese Tetsu Yamauchi to replace Lane. At this time Rod announced his engagement to Dee Harrington.

Early photo of Rod Stewart.

Rod's newest solo album, 'Smiler,' was released. On the album was the song 'Mine For Me' written for Rod by Paul McCartney.

In 1975 Rod Stewart met Britt Ekland. Rod invited Dee Harrington to fly out to Los Angeles to join him. This was when he was seeing Britt Ekland. Rod's relationship with Dee Harrington ended when Dee saw the couple together in the Los Angeles Troubadour club.

In April of 1975 Rod Stewart decided to go into tax exile. He chose Los Angeles as his new base of operations. Rod sold his home in England and bought a $750,000 house in Holmby Hills, California. Rod's move to America was of concern to his old band, Faces, but the band experienced another blow when Ronnie Wood accepted a temporary place in The Rolling Stones to fill in the gap of departing Mick Taylor. Mick Jagger had told Rod that he would never try to steal Ronnie Wood from Faces, but now it looked like he was trying to do just that.

In the High Court in December 1974 a judge freed Rod from his Mercury contract. Earlier, Warner Brothers had paid Rod a large sum of money for him to join them as soon as he was out of his Mercury contract. The time had now come for Rod to sign with Warner Brothers. Billy Gaff negotiated Rod an unbelievable $25 million, ten-album contract with the record company.

Rod's next album, 'Atlantic Crossing,' (which represented his move from England to the United States) is released and is another smash for him. The album entered the British charts at number one and stayed there for nearly two months. In the U.S. it reached number nine.

Rod finally makes the decision to leave Faces. Billy Gaff got the word from Rod first, then he telephoned The Daily Mirror and had them interview Rod over the telephone from his home in Los Angeles. December 19, 1975 the newspaper ran the headline on their front page 'Why Rock Star Rod is Quitting Faces.' The final nail to the coffin of the Faces' future came from Ronnie Wood when he announced on the same day of the article that he was joining The Rolling Stones on a permanent basis. Rod also would make an incredible larger amount of money from his solo touring compared to his days with Faces.

1976 saw the release of Rod's latest album 'A Night On The Town' which contained the controversial song 'The Killing of George (Parts I & II). The album also contained the smash hit 'Tonight's the Night' which became Rod's biggest hit to date in the U.S. Another first with the album was that it was on Rod's own record label, Riva. Billy Gaff who had stayed on board after the split with Faces was now Rod's personal manager and involved with Rod's record company and other business dealings.

In August of 1977, after a two year relationship, Rod and Britt Ekland broke up. It has been reported that Britt asked for a $12 million settlement for helping with Rod's career. The suit was eventually settled out of court.

In March of 1978 Rod began a relationship with Alana Hamilton, the former wife of actor George Hamilton. The couple married on April 6, 1979 which created news around the world. Two children were born within the marriage. In 1981 the British newspapers were writing about problems in the Alana and Rod Marriage.

In the Spring of 1982 Rod Stewart and his manager, Billy Gaff, separated because of business differences. The breakup went to court with millions of dollars at stake and was settled out of court.

1983 saw more newspaper stories of the problems storming up in Alana and Rod's marriage.

Rod's next two albums 'Body Wishes' in 1983, and 'Camouflage' in 1984 presented some problems for the performer. Very much disco flavored and weak material hurt his credibility as an artist and as a writer. Perhaps he listened to wrong advice on the choice of material and the style to present it in. Long time fans were hoping that Rod would come to his senses once again and give them material of his caliber and ability. Jim Cregan, Rod's longtime guitarist, stated in Ray Coleman's book, "I think we fell victim to the synthesized, drum-machine-driven, strange kind of record that didn't reflect Rod's roots....He seemed to have been derailed into an effort to sound rhythmically trendy...." It also probably didn't help that someone decided that Rod should have a new producer who turned out to be Michael Omartian, alumnus of Donna Summer's school of music. Unbelievablely, the album went to number five in Britain and thirty in the U.S.

At the start of 1984 Rod Stewart and Alana Hamilton's marriage was over. It was painful for Rod because of the two children involved. In the spring of 1984 Rod was being seen in public with a successful model by the name of Kelly Emberg. They would have a daughter together three years later.

In the summer of 1986 Rod performed again in England after a three year absence. What made the appearance even more memorable was that his backing band was Faces. Bandmate Ronnie Lane was there in a wheelchair having contacted multiple sclerosis.

Early Rod Stewart.

Bill Wyman from The Rolling Stones filled in for Lane on bass. Rods' new album was also released at this time. Titled 'Every Beat of My Heart' in England, and simply 'Rod Stewart' in the U.S. It went to the number two position in England.

In two years Rod was back out with his new album 'Out of Order' and a new world tour. The album and the tour did especially well in the U.S. and once more established Rod as a valid artist after his critically disappointing albums 'Body Wishes' and 'Camouflage.'

John Gray commented in Ray Coleman's book, after having met Rod Stewart for the first time at Stewart's local pub in Epping, "I could never imagine, say, David Bowie being as down to earth or as friendly. In the pub, with people going up to him for autographs, he always made conversation, found the time to talk."

In 1990 Rod's father passed away. It was also the year that he met a new lady friend by the name of Rachel Hunter. Hunter was a top English model who had moved to the USA. Rod first spotted her on a CNN cable television Sports Illustrated ad. Shortly after first seeing her on TV Rod met her at a Hollywood nightclub. In six short weeks after their first meeting they became engaged. Kelly Emberg and Rod's daughter Ruby moved out of Rod's house. December 15, 1990 Rod Stewart and Rachel Hunter were married. June 1, 1992 Rachel gave birth to a daughter, Renee. September 4, 1944 Rachel gave birth to a son, Liam.

On February 5, 1993 Rod was at Universal Studios to film and record what was to be called 'Unplugged...Seated.' Joining him and his eleven-piece band was Ronnie Wood. 'Unplugged...Seated' was a huge success. It entered the U.S. album charts at number two, and in the UK it also reached number two in the charts. It seemed that the world couldn't keep Rod Stewart down until something that happened to him in 1999.

Rachel Hunter left Rod. Rod could not believe it and kept expecting Rachel to return to him at any time. But she didn't. Rachel Hunter told the 'E' Entertainment cable television program, which did a program on her, that she left not because of any differences between her and Rod, but that she had seen a 'bag lady' going about her business and it made her wonder what she would be doing when she was eighty years old. She said that she was so young when she married and had the two children so quickly that she hadn't even had the time to find herself yet. Rod was devastated. Fans saw the visible sadness in Rod at his concerts, at least Rachel hadn't left Rod for another man. Rod had always left others for someone else, now someone had left him and it hurt.

Smiler, Issue #60, had some interesting material concerning the breakup, "Rod recently revealed how he turned to God after his split from Rachel. He was so depressed after the breakdown of his nine year marriage that his doctor suggested he take Prozac. Eventually, Rod decided to pray when he hit an all-time low five months ago. Rod told the Scottish Daily Record: 'I felt so frustrated, so unhappy, so miserable, I didn't know what to do. I just lay down on the bed and said to God 'Please, please, help me.' Now I don't think I've been as happy in my life. I know it is because God has come into my life. I think God has helped."

As of this writing The Toronto Star, May 31, 2000, reported this news, "Los Angeles (Reuters) - Veteran rocker Rod Stewart, whose gritty voice has helped him sell millions of records over a 30-year career, recently underwent thyroid surgery to remove a nod ule, his spokesman said Tuesday. The operation, which took place May 12th at Cedars-Sinai Medical Center in Los Angeles, was successful, and 55-year-old Stewart has been given a clean bill of health, said Paul Freundlich of public relations firm Rogers & Cowan.

The surgery took place following a routine CAT scan that revealed a nodule in the right lobe of Stewart's thyroid gland. Doctors operated to make sure the nodule was benign. The singer's vocal cords were unaffected by the procedure, Freundlich added. His statement added that the football-mad Stewart played in a charity match in England last Saturday, and the rocker is also finishing an album set for release this fall. Stewart, currently enjoying the single life after his 1999 split from second wife Rachel Hunter, is best known for such hit songs as 'Maggie Mae,' 'Tonight's the Night' and 'DaYa Think I'm Sexy?'"

There have been reports that Rod and Rachel have been seen together. Each of them have had cancer scares, perhaps these circumstances have brought them together? Rod's fans will just have to wait and see what happens in the future. One thing is for sure and that is that Rod's future is bound to be as exciting as his past has been.

* * *

Interview with Rod Stewart's Sister, Mary Cady

Thanks to the Smiler staff, John Gray, Marilyn Kennedy and Rita Belcher for their help in getting this interview with Rod's sister. And thanks to Mary for consenting to this interview.

* * *

Question: Was the family concerned about Rod when he left school at fifteen with no educational certificates?

Mary: We were very worried.

Question: During Rod's beatnik/gypsy days when he was sixteen, seventeen (before he started with Long John Baldry) what did you think would become of Rod?

Mary: We didn't know what was going to happen to him. It was a very worrying time for us.

Question: Rod found his element and gift in music. What do you think Rod would have become if it was not music?

Mary: No idea at all, possibly he would have tried to become a footballer.

Question: Did you see Rod perform in the early days?

Mary: The first time I saw him was at the London Palladium with Steampacket. They were support to the Stones. I did think he'd be successful but he has gone way beyond my expectations.

Question: It's been written that when Rod was with The Jeff Beck Group was when his voice started to change. What do you think brought that about?

Mary: No idea at all.

Question: It seems that during Rod's album 'Every Picture Tells A Story' that he first became a millionaire. Did you notice any change in Rod after this success?

Mary: There was no change in him then and there is no change now. He is still my baby brother.

Question: What were your feelings when Rod relocated to the U.S.?

Mary: It was very upsetting for our parents. They were heartbroken. They wondered when they would see him again.

Question: What do you think of Rod's many marriages?

Mary: He has ONLY BEEN MARRIED TWICE. It's just one of those things. They didn't work out. It happens to a lot of people.

Question: Many people say that Rod is very good to his fans. Can you comment on this, or do you have any stories to share?

Mary: Yes, he is very good to his fans. He helps out when he can and has a lot of patience. Never minds signing an autograph.

Question: What are some of your fondest memories of Rod?

Mary: More than anything when he bought the house in Windsor. He took me to have a look at it. He lay flat on his back with his arms and legs in the air shouting, "It's All Mine." I wish I'd had a camera to take a picture.

Question: What are some of your pet peeves about Rod?

Mary: He likes his own way.

Question: What do you think are Rod's strongest points?

Mary: He loves his children and his family. His children especially.

Question: What does the family now think of Rod when he plays concerts like the recent 1999 televised one in Scotland? What goes through your mind?

Mary: Just so proud. Can't believe it's him where he is. It's hard to take it in.

Question: Elvis had always wondered why he had become so famous and successful. He always asked himself, "Why did I have this ability?" Do you ever think that Rod was given his gift of music, that brings joy to millions, and that this is his destiny?

Mary: Yes, he loves to perform.

Memorable Quotes from Rod Stewart & Friends

Thanks to Smiler Magazine for the permission to use these quotes from their Issue # 50 which ran under the headline of 'Recorded Highlights & Action Replays, A nostalgic look at classic Smiler interview quotes.'

"Last time I saw John [Peel] was just before one of the Wembley Arena concerts last year. If it wasn't for John Peel the Faces would have never broke through. He single-handedly broke the Faces. John used to have lots of trouble trying to get us out of the pub, because his show was live and we had to go on the air at 7:30 and 7:25 we'd still be in the pub! There would be sweat pouring down his face trying to get us out! I think that's why he went bald."

- **Rod Stewart: May 22, 1987, Issue 12**

"There is only one Ron Wood and I'm nowhere near replacing him. I'm Rod's mate and we're probably as close as he was with Woody when we're working together. However, that camaraderie that the Faces had and the silliness that Rod and Ron had together, I wouldn't even attempt to duplicate."

- **Jim Cregan: August 7, 1987, Issue 15**

"I went to one of Rod's Earls Court concerts [1983], it was a big tartan do. I can remember because I always thought he couldn't sing off-key, but he managed to sing off-key most of the way through that. It really was bad, I was surprised, I always assumed that he had one of those natural voices where he couldn't get it wrong if he wanted to."

- **John Peel: January 13, 1988, Issue 15**

"I don't want to get typecast by making Rock 'n' Roll records all the time. I want to break away from it, I've got so many ideas. I want to go back to the States and make an album with just acoustic instruments, like 'Every Picture Tells A Story.' I see guys like John Cougar Mellencamp and Bruce Springsteen doing it, and I was the first, so I want to do something like that again."

- **Rod Stewart: May 30, 1988, Issue 16**

"Rod used to work on a week to week basis and we'd record about one track a week. Rod would decide what number he wanted to do, and if Martin [Quittenton] or Ronnie [Wood] or I were involved, we'd go over to his house in Windsor and work it out. A week or two later we'd do another one. That's the way he made albums in those days."

- **Micky Waller: April 17, 1989, Issue 20**

"I don't get asked to sing live [on television] anymore, the people involved don't want the technical problems of setting up a live mic. I just do what I'm asked. I could sing live, but it's easier to do a backing track because I haven't got to worry about my voice being in tune."

- Rod Stewart: March 4, 1990, Issue 23

"Rod wore the stage clothes during the day. Ronnie Lane hated it so much, there was a dreadful bust up and he called Rod an aging Queen! Ronnie couldn't bear to be associated with anyone who wore those kind of clothes."

- Dee Harrington: July 20, 1990, Issue 25

"I would walk through a brick wall for Rod and, in turn, he would do anything for the family. He's never given us hand-outs. As his family, people seem to think we should be millionaires too. What I've got, I've worked for, the same as Mary and Bob. Rod has always looked after my mother and father very very well, you couldn't ask for more. I've been all over the world with him and its never cost me a penny, although sometimes I think he's a bit of a tight bugger!"

- Don Stewart: January 29, 1991, Issue 27

"You usually know if you've got a couple of hit singles, but you never know if the album is going to sell. If you've got one or two hit singles, they usually help to sell an album but not necessarily. Take 'Love

Touch' which was a huge, huge hit in the States, but the album only did about 200,000."

- **Rod Stewart: January 2, 1992, Issue 30**

"Rod and I were incredibly frustrated when it came to recording with Faces. Rod and I were never on anything, we just used to drink. Everybody else in the band took a lot of other things and we were always night owls. Rod and I would have preferred to have gone in the studio at eleven or twelve in the morning. Really it was the Faces, in house, that let themselves down when it came to recording."

- **Kenny Jones: September 1, 1992, Issue 33**

"During the seventies I was going through a really heavy situation and at that particular time Rod was like a crutch for me. It was at the time he was with Britt and he helped me enormously. He was there for me when I needed him. We'd known each other a long time before that, but I was going through a hellish time. Rod was there and he went out of his way, which was wonderful."

- **Long John Baldry: March 6, 1993, Issue 35**

"The resentment set in for me when we were billed as Rod Stewart and The Faces. That was Billy Gaff's fault, and maybe Rod's, I don't know. That was when I fired Billy Gaff as my manager, because there was no need for that. You don't see Mick Jagger and The Rolling Stones or John Lennon and The Beatles."

- **Ian Mclagan: November 2, 1993, Issue 38**

"If you jump around and look stupid as though you can't do it anymore, then you'll have problems. But if you look athletic, very strong and powerful, they can't say a ###t to you. Half the critics hate what Rod can do anyway - he still runs around the stage, and sings better than ever."

- Carmine Rojas: February 17, 1994, Issue 40

"I don't know what happened to 'Lead Vocalist.' It all finished up in a heap of ###t really, because there were some good things that escaped. I don't know how that came about, it ruined the album. I don't think people wanted to hear those old Faces things again. Actually, it didn't help the 'Unplugged' album either, because we released two albums in the space of three months and record companies have their budgets."

- Rod Stewart: September 14, 1994, Issue 41

"I couldn't just sit around all day doing nothing. It's alright for a month, but I need to work. I realize maybe I won't be able to do this forever. I just like to get out and play. Anybody will tell you who has ever been on stage, in any shape or form, it's very addictive. It's a lovely way to earn a living, it really is - I love it."

- Rod Stewart: July 24, 1996, Issue 49

* * *

Fan's Stories
and
Concert Reviews

Here is a collection of various fan's stories, encounters with Rod and concert reviews by fans. All of these are interesting not just for the stories, but what they show us about the fans and what they show us about Rod himself. Hope you enjoy the hidden treasures they reveal.

* * *

"My son Tyler has grown up on Rod since day one, so its only natural that he would be a big Rod fan just like his mom. He went to his first concert before he was even born (I was 7 months pregnant). From the time he learned to speak, he was trying to sing to Rod songs....and would walk around the house singing 'Hot Legs'!

Once Tyler turned four and began to ask to go to concerts with me I decided I'd give it a try...of course everyone else thought I was nuts to even attempt to take a four year old to a rock concert! But I knew he'd be fine, especially since he spends so much time mimicking Rod and putting on concerts in our living room....even down to swinging the microphone like Rod.

The day of the show Tyler was filled with questions and anticipation. Where will our seats be? Can I sing onstage with Rod? Can I get a soccer ball? Well, being a long time fan I know firsthand how hard it is to get a soccer ball, let alone even think about being onstage (took me 20 years to get a ball, and I still haven't made it onstage!), I knew this would be near impossible. But being that it was his first show, there was no way I was going to disappoint him ahead of time by saying there is no way this will happen. So, instead I said, 'Well honey, you can only get on stage IF Rod says you can.' And this answer seemed to appease him. Tyler wanted to take his microphone with him to the show....which in reality is not a real microphone, but my camcorder tripod! He extends it to make it like Rod's microphone and tilts up the handle to sing into, and unscrews the handle if Rod uses his cordless microphone. With much convincing, I persuaded him to only take the cordless mic (the handle) due to space limitations. Tyler's father was concerned about the loudness of the show and got him some earplugs to wear; and since Tyler thought they looked like the ones Rod uses he was eager to use them.

Once at the show we were thrilled to find that our seats were front row center, thanks to the help of Smiler! Tyler sat atop my shoulders and sang every song right along with Rod....holding his mic in one hand and waving with the other one. Everyone from

Little Tyler Deaton on stage with Rod Stewart At Charlotte, North Carolina.

security, the band and even Rod seemed as impressed with this little four year old as he was of them. They couldn't seem to get over how he was so into the show....and they all made the show special to him by all the attention they showered him with. Now if the night had ended there it would've still been a great memory for Tyler....front row, a great show, and being noticed by Rod and the band; but this was only the beginning.

As the show came closer to the end 'Having A Party' started and some girls from the right of the stage were allowed up to dance on the stage, and without even thinking about it I mouthed to Freddie, 'Can you get him up on stage?' not even knowing if he'd understand, or be willing to do it. And without hesitation Freddie said 'C'mon,' and motioned us to the far left of the stage where he met us and helped Tyler up on the stage! Security didn't allow me up with him, but without hesitation Tyler went off across the stage with Freddie, and right up to Rod. Rod knelt down, put his arm around Tyler, and the next thing I know they are up on the big screens nose to nose with each of them singing into their microphones.

As the song was finishing up Rod gave Tyler a soccer ball, but Tyler gave Rod a surprise! Tyler thought Rod was giving it to him to kick out into the audience like he does....so he kicks it to the crowd! The look of shock on Rod's face was priceless! Luckily, thanks to those big speakers and some help from the band, the ball never made it to the crowd, and they let Tyler know it was for him to keep. Before we knew it the song was over and Freddie was bringing him back to me at the edge of the stage. It was a unbelievable night....all of Tyler's dreams came true that night: front row, onstage with Rod and the band and a soccer ball ALL in the same show. From that night on Tyler was definitely hooked.

After the show we called and left Rita a message in New York thanking her for Smiler's help in getting the awesome tickets. I didn't get to speak directly to her so I decided to wait and call her at home that next week after she returned from the Smiler party. When I did catch up with her to tell her about Tyler's night.... she already knew the details. I was dumbfounded because I knew I didn't leave all that on her message. Well, to my surprise she heard about it from Don and Mary (Rod's brother and sister) at the Smiler party! They had attended the Charlotte show on their way to New York for the Smiler gathering, and had watched Tyler off and on throughout the show. In fact, it was Rod's brother and sister who were responsible for him getting his soccer ball!

The Charlotte '98 show will always be one of the most precious concert memories to me, and definitely a story I'm sure Tyler will look back on and tell his children one day."

- Cathy Deaton

* * *

"My story begins in the early 90's when my husband, Gary, as a surprise, bought two tickets to see Rod Stewart in concert. We really didn't go to many concerts at this point because the 80's kept us busy raising our two daughters, and he thought this would be nice for us to "get away" for the weekend. We made some reservations and off we went. Our seats were nowhere near the stage, in fact I had to use my binoculars! The show was great and at the end when I saw Rod pull a few girls on stage - I ALMOST DIED! I looked at my husband and said how cool that would

Kathy Hurd on stage with Rod.

Kathy Hurd with Rod.

be to be pulled up on stage. At this point, we both decided that these seats SUCKED. The show ended and off we went to our hotel.

As time went on, we went to a couple more Rod shows and managed to get closer to the stage. In 1994 I heard on the radio that tickets were going on sale for Rod in Cleveland. I called a ticket broker and paid quite a bit for 8th row. The day of the concert, I bought a single rose. The show started and it was very hard to get close to the stage. The show was in the round and Rod was all over the place - he was INCREDIBLE! I was still holding this rose and watched as everyone was throwing them on the stage. I told my husband - I paid five bucks for this damn rose and I am going to personally hand it to Rod. We took our coats and started walking around the stage as if we were leaving. As we walked along, suddenly Rod came right to the end of the stage where we were standing. All I could think of was GO! NOW!!! GIVE ROD THE ROSE !!!!!! What perfect timing. As I held my hand up to give the rose to Rod, I kept it there only to touch him. All of a sudden, Rod grabbed my hand and UP I WENT!! It was 'Twistin'' and there I was - ME & ROD! He had his arm around my shoulders as he sang. It was the greatest moment. I couldn't believe this was happening to me. Rod saw my husband below with the camera and even posed for a picture (the two of us). Rod was about half way done with the song and all of a sudden girls were jumping up on the stage everywhere. Rod was running in all directions from the girls until he was taken off stage and the show was over. I was on this high for almost two days. I was so excited when I developed my pictures.

Rod was playing the following week in Pittsburgh. I HAD TO GO!! I was able to get some tickets to the show and my husband and I went again. We managed to get close to the stage and at the end when Rod pulled a girl on stage, he saw me and motioned to me to "come up." It happened again! I was on stage for a second time with Rod.

Rod was not touring again until 1996. From Connecticut to New York, New Jersey to Philly and Chicago, we had quite a few "get away" weekends. My husband and I have met some really neat people from going to Rod's concerts, who we still get together with before and after the shows.

In 1997, about five of us decided to attend a Smiler Party in England. What an experience! We were hoping Rod might surprise us and show up at the party for a few minutes. Well, the next best thing to having Rod at the party would be to have his brother Don and sister Mary! What a BLAST! I even had the pleasure of dancing with Don! What an exciting night.

As we attended more and more shows, we were very fortunate and lucky to have front row at so many of Rod's concerts. I made Rod several gifts - from vests to shirts to banners and plaques. In return, I have five soccer balls, of which Rod personally handed me three. His music has given us so much enjoyment, including relaxation and many new friends in the past 10 years.

Because of the number of shows we have gone to, we've had the pleasure of meeting the band and crew members. They are all SUPER!!!

From 1990 - 1999 I've lost count of the shows we've attended. I do know that this millennium has started off the best possible way it could for Gary and I - having spent New Years Eve at the Rio on stage with Rod and also experiencing Rod at a Rodeo in February. It certainly has been exciting. A special thanks to all the guys in the band - hope to see you soon....down in front."

       - Kathy & Gary Hurd

       * * *

"The Best Night of My Life" by Jo Wilhelm

"The day before Rod Stewart's concert (March 29, 1996) here in St. Louis at the Keil Center I called a friend of mine, Roche Madden, who is a new reporter for Fox, Channel 2, KTVI. I told him that I had second row seats for the concert and asked him if he could possibly get me backstage passes. My boyfriend, Kenny, had gotten us the second row seats and I could not believe my great fortune because I had never before been able to be this close to Rod, the very best singer, songwriter and performer ever! Roche said he would talk to his boss and see what he could do about the backstage passes.

Since it was already noon on the day of the concert, I figured I would not be hearing back from Roche and I went out to have my nails done in gold to match the black and gold outfit I had bought for the concert.

Around 3:00 pm the phone rang and it was Roche. He asked me what my address was and said that he was on his way with a cameraman to do a special interest story about me being one of Rod's biggest fans.

I was frantic because I was not dressed, had no makeup on and the only housework I had done that day was to make the bed. My boyfriend was rushing around like crazy putting some of my collection on the couch, throwing things in closets and trying to get the house in some kind of order while I was getting ready.

They were here for about three hours asking me questions and filming me and every room of my house since I have Rod memorabilia scattered around everywhere. When they were finished Roche said to meet him and his cameraman at the Keil Center at 7:00. We called several friends and family and told them to watch and/or tape the 10:00 o'clock news that night, plus we put a blank VCR tape in before we left, 'just in case.'

Roche filmed me going into the Keil Center and when I handed in my ticket to the ticket taker they asked if they could follow me in to my second row seat. But the Kiel personnel said that they could not come past the ticket taker. They had wanted to try to film me giving a special bouquet to Rod that I had made up at a floral shop.

At the beginning of the concert Rod walked over to where I was standing, looked right at me and took the black, gold and white bouquet from me (these were the colors on 'A Spanner In The Works,' his latest album at the time). He held it for awhile and then laid it down in the center of the stage.

Toward the end of the concert he stepped down from the stage, surrounded by several security people, and when he came my way he stopped and looked right at me again. I was able to put my right hand on the left hand upper pocket of the yellow jacket he was wearing. I was totally stunned!

The rest of the concert was like no other one I have ever been to, and I have been to over 300 of them in my life. Not even seeing the Beatles could come close to his! I spent almost all of the time standing and being pushed into the fence around the stage so I could be as close as possible to Rod, and in two inch

Jo Wilhelm with Rod. Not really,
Just with a 'Rod' stand-up!

Some of Jo Wilhelm's 'Rod' collection.

More of Jo Wilhelm's collection.

heels! I was shoved, stepped on, pushed and was so close I could even see Rod sweat. I left the concert hardly able to walk, my voice was almost gone from singing along and cheering. I was soaking wet from my head to my toes from dancing and moving with the music as much as I could in my tiny space where I felt like a sardine, but I loved every second of it!

After I dragged myself in the house along with my boyfriend we found that there were several messages on my answering machine about how good I looked on TV. The two of us collapsed and we watched the tape of why this night was one of the most important, unforgettable, wonderful and memorable in my life.

My boyfriend was able to get 26 photos at Rod's concert. I had them enlarged and thanks to Marilyn Kennedy and Rita Belcher's help Rod personalized and autographed my favorite one. I have to thank Rod (like he thanks Muddy, Sam and Otis) for bringing so much joy and happiness to me through his music and for all the dynamic energy he has put into it."

* * *

"About Rod Stewart" by Sean Thomas

"Rod is like an angel who always makes me happy with his songs. When I was little my mom played Rod's music all the time. I heard other music on the radio too, but Rod just stuck to me. I haven't heard anybody else who sings as great as Rod does. I think he has done more excellent songs than any other singer. Four years ago I was 7 years old and I got very upset because my mom didn't take me to see Rod when he came here. But then she didn't know how much I loved him. When she found out she took me to see Rod for 2 shows in New York City, a few months

Rod delighting the fans.

Concert poster that the author designed. Rod said it was the best poster he had seen in 15 years.

'Out of Order' Tour. The Tulsa, April 19th, 1989 concert.

'Out of Order' Tour, April 19, 1989 Tulsa, concert.

Rachel Proctor giving Rod a "Kicks" soccer beanie baby at Burghettstown, PA (Rod gave Rachel an autographed soccer ball in return).

More of Jo Wilhelm's Rod Stewart Collection.

More of Jo Wilhelm's collection.

Rachel Hunter with Rod Stewart.

later. It was my first Rod concert and after that I couldn't get enough of Rod. I remember I cried after the concerts because I was afraid I would never see him again. I have though - 11 more times.

Rod's concerts are awesome. He is so energetic and is really nice to the audience. He looks like he appreciates and loves his fans. Sometimes he even lets people come on stage with him. I got to do that 3 times. The first time was in New York City in 1998. I danced with Rod and 6 other people while he sang 'Havin' A Party.' Then in 1999 I got to dance right next to Rod in Mansfield. This time there were a lot of other people on stage. When he was done with the song, Rod patted me on the head when we left the stage. I came off the stage shaking. And in Cleveland in 1999 Rod invited everybody to come on the stage for his encore! I got up there, but not everyone could fit. But that was really wonderful for him to do that.

I went to see Rod in Toronto in March 1999. I gave him a gift. I was so excited because he looked at it and smiled and I KNEW he liked it. That made me so happy. Then he motioned for me to wait a minute and then tossed a soccer ball right to me. Getting a soccer ball right from Rod was one of the best moments in my life. I even slept with it that night.

It is because of Rod I got to meet the nicest people in the world. They are his fans. I even got an extra 'mom' when I met Ms. Rita. She is the U.S. Secretary for Smiler and she is so great to me and everyone. All of Rod's fans I've met are super!

My mom loves Rod just like I do so we know how cool it is to share and talk about Rod. She takes me a lot of places for Rod concerts and that is so wonderful of her to do for me. What's excellent is that I know my mom really understands when I get excited about Rod things.

Sometimes I really wish that I had been born sooner because I missed so many years that Rod performed. But I am very lucky that I still can enjoy the best singer ever, Rod Stewart!"

* * *

The following is a reply that I received from Rita, the U.S. Rep for Smiler. I had learned that Rita has trouble with her bad, so bad that many nights she only gets a few hours of sleep. I had asked her how she copes with this terrible problem.

"How do I cope? Ummmm good question. When you are diagnosed with a disease that causes chronic pain you can handle it one of two ways. Number one, you can sit around and feel sorry for yourself, or number two, you can fight it and I'm a fighter. Sometimes it's not always easy especially if I've gone a few weeks with hardly any sleep. This Smiler job has been a blessing in more ways than one. On the nights when I'm back up after getting a couple hours sleep, I've always got work to do to keep my mind off the pain. As for having inner sources, I would have to say Rod's music is one of them. When I'm having a really bad day, I ALWAYS listen to 'Never Give Up On A Dream' and the words to that song will remind me how much of a fighter I am. I know that probably sounds corny, but it's true. Thank you for your kind words, they mean a lot."

* * *

American Music Awards, 1-22-90.

A young Rod Stewart.

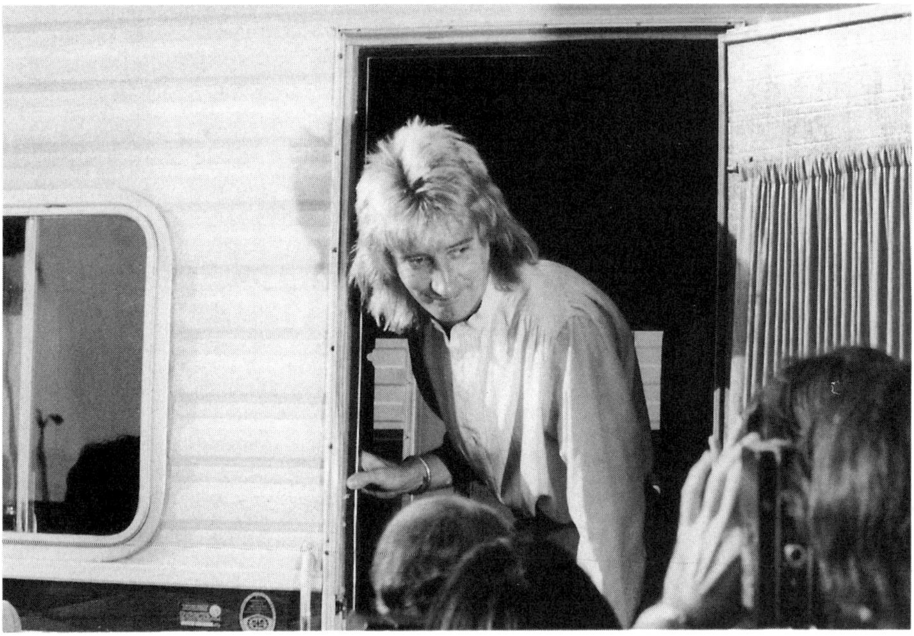

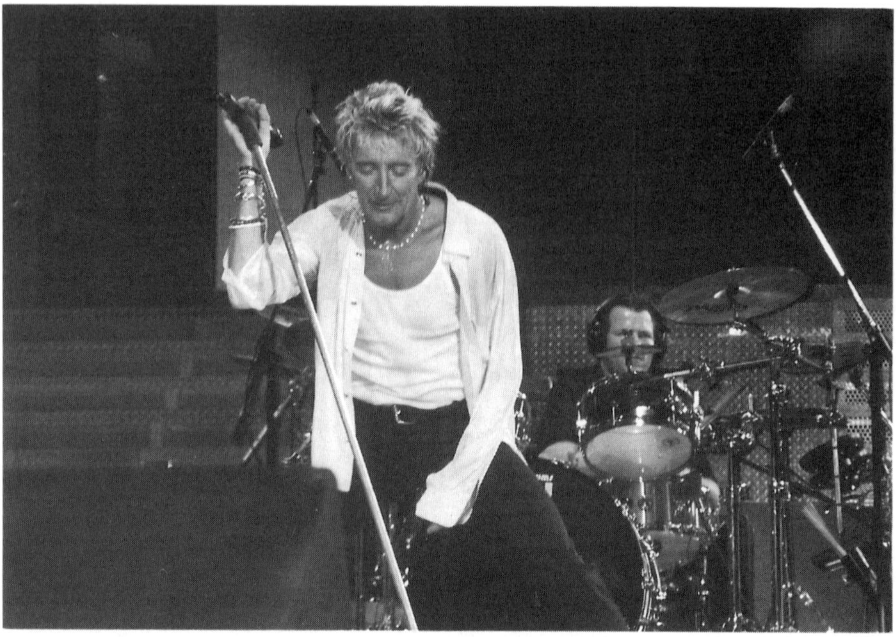

63

"Rod Stewart" by Shannon M. Holliker

"It is 4:30 am on another weekday. The alarm clock blares the sounds of the deejays announcing the morning traffic report, it's time for the snooze button once again. 5:00 am welcomes the new day with the sounds of the alarm clock again. The seemingly two second intervals has actually allowed for 30 extra minutes of rest between the haze of reality and the dream world. This time is different, the song on the radio is 'A Reason To Believe.' I open my eyes quickly as if I am hearing it for the first time. I continue to lay peacefully listening to the words filling my head with thoughts of Rod Stewart. This, I don't have to convince myself, is worth opening my eyes for.

So what is this magic spell Rod has once again put over me? It is not a typical compassion of a singer as fellow fans can tell you. We are the priviledged few who have a deep understanding of what legends are truly made of. I can say his name with the same enthusiasm this time that I had many years ago when I was first introduced to him. I was a baby, a mere three years old when I first heard his unmistakable voice playing on the radio. I was addicted, I am a Rodaholic.

My whole life transformed when I went to my first Rod concert. I gazed speechlessly at Rod and his superhero like performance. I had never seen a sight that breathtaking in all of my life. It was virtually amazing. My collection of memorabilia grew bigger by the day. By my Senior year of high school, my life centered around Rod Stewart. I wanted to expose everyone to the joy of his music. I researched his life for over four months to create the best tribute that I could think of. My Senior exit project was a twenty minute oral-video presentation compiled primarily of

Rod's greatest accomplishments. Now, as I brush the shoulders of those I graduated with years later, I'm told that whenever they hear a Rod song on the radio that they think of me.

Rod fans possess the unique ability to relate every one of his songs to a significant part of our own lives. We are content with the simple pleasure a Rod album brings. Just one of his songs could play continuously over and over and we would never tire from it. The best appreciation of who Rod is comes from really listening to him, and hearing that special sound that fellow fans hear. It is truly a connection like no other.

The name Rod Stewart screams the word 'genuine.' We all have some darkness where we have light. Rod is no different, he is not untouchable. He is as human as any one of us. His climb has been a struggle from the beginning. He has not fallen victim to fear, and in return he has conquered his dreams. In reflection of his life as a 'storyteller,' I admire Rod. His persistence and dedication have returned to him with internal success. He has yet to fall short of a dream. He has taught me that if I fall to get up and keep climbing. I have many dreams, and goals that will not be easily reached. I know that I will be able to do it as long as I refuse to fall.

I am always asked what I would do if I got to meet Rod in person. I would just simply thank him for what he has given me. I had my closest encounter at an amazing concert in 1999. I sat third row from the stage, where there was quite a bit of communication through gestures during his performance. He pointed out my handmade 'Rod hat' to fellow band members as they shared a few laughs. The best night of my life was rewarded with a soccer ball that he tossed over to me. We all dream of meeting Rod one day. There is one sure way because he is much closer than I once imagined. The first time I met Rod was when I layed down in a quiet room. I closed my eyes and played 'Sailing.' He puts his heart, soul and spirit into each performance. It was then that I realized I had finally met the true Rod Stewart.

As 'A Reason To Believe' came to an end, I got up to begin my day. Thirty minutes later than I am suppose to. I gently came back from my reflections of my special Rod thoughts. The dreadful thought of my job began to take over. I pulled out my CD from my collection, pressed the play button and got in the shower. Rod was filling the air again. I refused to let my job get the best of me. Today, I will refuse to fall to defeat, I tell myself. I know that this job is merely a stepping stone on my way to fulfilling my dreams. I have chosen to keep climbing, because thanks to Mr. Stewart I have found "a reason to believe."

* * *

"I have been a Rod Stewart fan since the first time I heard 'Do Ya Think I'm Sexy?' in 1978. I was in the 4th grade and taking roller skating lessons. Every Wednesday after school for weeks, I would request it to be played. I don't know what it was about the song, maybe the music, maybe the voice, probably the combination of the two, but I was hooked. That was a lot of years ago and so much has changed and so much has stayed the same in my journey as a Rod fan. I still hear "Why?" as in "Why do you go out of your way to see Rod?" "Why have you put yourself through all of that and you've never even met him?" and the like. In the 22 years Rod's music has been in my life I still can't completely answer those questions. What I can do is give you my perspective on what it has been like having Rod as part of my life for so long and let you try to figure out "Why."

I think music is a medium that we all use and respond to help us express and identify emotions when we can't find the right words. We all hear a song and remember significant moments in our lives, good and bad. That rang true for me in junior high and high school. Adolescence is such a time of changing, developing, winning, losing and rebelling. I felt like I could really relate to Rod's lyrics and that in every situation he knew exactly what I was thinking. My friends didn't really get into Rod so most of the time I listened to his music alone. In some ways, it was like a friendship was developing. Just me and Rod. He could cheer me up, make me laugh, or make me cry with just the touch of the play button on the cassette player. Probably my biggest regret is that I never got to see Rod in concert during those years. I grew up in a small town that Rod wouldn't ever have come to and the closest cities were a few hours away. I'm sure my parents would not have let me go anyway!

I went off to college in 1985 and just by chance met a girl who liked Rod, too. I'll never forget our first conversation. We had been discussing music in general and she asked me if I listened to Rod. Since she was African-American, I didn't think she would have paid that much attention to Rod's music. In turn, she was surprised that I knew anything at all about Sam Cooke, Muddy Waters, Otis Redding and the other greats who were Rod's influences, seeing that I was Caucasian. We laugh about that now and she is still one of my best friends! Finally, finding another person who felt like I did about Rod intensified my feelings toward my 'hobby', I guess you would have called it then. My friend is quite a historian and she and I have spent literally countless hours talking about all things Rod, learning about his life, his influences and trying to tease out the truth from the rumors and flat out lies. Going off to college put me a lot closer to venues where Rod played and I was finally able to see Rod in person during the Out of Order tour! My friend and I called for tickets and were only able to get lawn seats, but you would have thought we were front row with how excited we were! But, that excitement paled in comparison to the moment the curtain dropped and we set eyes on Rod, from way back on the lawn, for the first time. That was an exhilaration that I had never felt before, but still feel each and every time the curtain falls. That first time, though, underneath the exhilaration, was a feeling that I had been reunited with a long time friend.

It was such a special time for me as a fan from that concert on until I met Smiler members online in 1995. I had no 'connections' to get us front row tickets, no special relationship with anyone who could get us backstage, no money to pay ticket scalpers, and no clue how to start. It was just the love and respect of Rod and his music that kept us coming back. It was just that simple. I listened to the radio from home and work and school, day and night, trying to win tickets but never did. We tried the approach of calling for tickets. Most of the time, we had phones to each ear, dialing different TicketMaster numbers for hours trying to get through. By this time, my sister had joined on as a fan and we spent some freezing nights sleeping out for tickets at the venues. I remember once we set up lawn chairs in freezing rain and waited in line from 10:00 pm until tickets went on sale the next morning, covered with plastic tarps, holding umbrellas over us to try to keep us dry. When it became unbearable, we took turns going to the car to keep warm. We still never got decent tickets. When the initial disappointment wore off, and let me tell you, that disappointment had me in tears numerous times, the excitement was still the same. At least we were there!

Probably one of the most stressful nights of my life

was trying to get to a Rod show. To understand the full effect, you need to realize that I am terrified of driving in the snow. Well, there was a blizzard the day of the show. I was at work and had to drive 30 minutes to pick up my friend who had a broken leg and was in a cast, drive 45 minutes back to my apartment to pick up my sister, then drive another 30 minutes to the venue. I told my supervisor I was sick and left work early. I was a nervous wreck when I got to my friend's apartment but we started back to get my sister. We made it home, but were running late and I was shaking, nauseous, and almost in tears. It was dark and you couldn't see two feet in front of you with all the snow. I begged my sister to drive to the show, but she wouldn't as she was also worried about the weather. It didn't even occur to me not to go to the concert and we started back to the venue. On the exit ramp about a mile from the venue, my driver's side windshield wiper flew off my car and I was instantly blinded as the snow was falling so thick and heavy. By some miracle, I had a long-handled snow brush under my seat and I rolled down my window and brushed the snow enough that I could see. We made it to the venue! Thank God Rod never starts on time! We asked a few people to help us with the windshield wiper, thinking we could switch the passenger side one to the driver's side, but no one could get it off. The minute we walked into the show, it was like the stress melted away. For two hours, I was transported away to my favorite place. I remember Rod thanking everyone for coming out in the nasty weather. After the show I called AAA and waited forever for them to come tow my car home. Nobody would help us. There were so many cars stuck and they had even shut down the highway. Security and maintenance told us they couldn't touch the car due to their policies. Can you imagine the tow truck driver, my sister, my friend in a leg cast, and me all stuffed in the cab of the truck! We were literally sitting on each other's laps. I called off work the next day. Would I do that again? You betcha!

In between tours, my friend and I would buy every magazine and videotaped every interview we could find. As soon as the interview was over, we would call each other to talk about it and critique the performance. We even had a Rod party once and stayed up 24 hours to watch all 24 hours of Rod on VH-1, repeats and all. Yes, we videotaped all 24 hours. We tried to contact Rod's management company to see if there was a fan club around, but never got a response. By this time, my network of family and friends also had their eyes open for anything Rod related. Friends would call to make sure I knew about whatever performance/interview. They would cut articles out of the paper or magazines for me. My parents and grandmother were even into it. My father watched the Unplugged show on MTV to 'see what this Rod Stewart was all about.' My parents even called me one day to tell me that a radio station in my hometown was having a bus trip to see Rod in Toronto. My sister and I drove the 2 hours home and my dad went with us to buy the tickets. Diane and I got the last two tickets! It sounds silly, but Rod being such a conversation piece has led to deepening friendships and relationships for me.

I have accidentally fallen asleep waiting for Rod's appearances on TV and have actually woken up the minute I heard Rod's voice. My boyfriend never quite understood this Rod connection and although he was great about listening to me go on and on, he did get angry with me once. I was waiting for Rod to be on the American Music Awards and my boyfriend was feeling amorous. I was tired and was about to fall asleep but I sat straight up in bed when Rod came on! My boyfriend should have been able to reap the benefits afterwards, but he was so mad at me he just went to bed. Aside from that day, my boyfriend and Rod were responsible for the most romantic nights of my life. One Valentine's Day, there was a concert broadcast on the radio. Let's just say that the music, a little wine, and my boyfriend made that a night to remember. My boyfriend only went to one concert with me. He was such a doll that night. It was the next concert after the snowstorm concert. He drove, paid for everything, and just kept saying, 'This is your night, honey. I love you.' He even enjoyed the show and didn't mind all of my singing and screaming. He eventually proposed to me and we agreed that we would dance to 'Broken Arrow' at our wedding.

In January 1995, my life changed dramatically. My boyfriend, who was then my fiance', died unexpectedly. This is still difficult to write about, but it needs to be said how Rod's music and several people involved with Smiler, my Rod Angels, helped my grieving process and made some dreams come true. At first, I couldn't listen to Rod at all because every single song reminded me of him and it hurt so much. But I realized that I had to go through the pain and express it before I could get any better, so I started listening. Sometimes I thought the tears would never stop and sometimes I thought I was going crazy, but even though it took a year before I could listen to 'Broken Arrow,' I was able to come to terms with what had happened and start to rebuild my life.

I made a decision to continue my graduate school program that I had begun just one week before my fiance' died. One of my classes required internet research and with the help of my professor, I was introduced to the Internet. I signed up with American Online at home and began to do searches. It seemed like second nature to do a Rod search and I posted a note somewhere asking for information about a fan club. I was surprised and thrilled to get a response from another fan who put me in touch with the fan club's USA secretary. I immediately joined Smiler and she introduced me to other Smiler members on a group email list. Overwhelmed doesn't come close to describing the next few months. The group emailed back and forth daily and I simply couldn't believe that there were so many people feeling exactly how I did about Rod and his music. There was an immediate connection and it seemed that I had known most of these people for years. I heard stories about how other people had met Rod, caught soccer balls, had front row seats and felt like finally I might find out how I could get decent seats. That October, we learned that the fan club president from England, John Gray, was coming to New York City and quite a group of us who had been talking online decided to go to NYC to meet him and to finally put names with faces. It was with great apprehension that I agreed to go. The fan club secretary picked up another fan in Toledo, came to Cleveland to pick me up, then it was off to Philadelphia to pick up another fan, and finally off to New Jersey to stay with another fan who we would then go into the city with to meet even more people. Everyone I talked to about this told me I was nuts to go off like that with people I had never met, I knew that and was scared but I went anyway. It was an incredible trip. It was like we had been friends forever. We swapped Rod stories, watched videos that I didn't know even existed, went to Greenwich Village and found bootleg CD's that I had no idea even existed and listened to John Gray talk about his experiences with Rod and Smiler. I thought I was going to die when we went to a place called Kennedy's and were shown a guitar autographed by Rod! There was a group dynamic present that just had to be experienced. All of us, so different, yet very much the same.

As time passed, our online group went through some changes and deeper friendships developed among a lot of us. As we prepared for the upcoming tour, Smiler was working hard to make premium tickets available for Smiler members. I couldn't imagine actually being able to see Rod up close, but it became a reality. For the first time, no sleeping out for tickets or calling for hours only to be stuck in the upper level. My first show, up close, was in Pittsburgh. I took my longtime Rod friend from college, my sister and another friend. As our tickets were held at will call, we had no idea where the tickets would be. They were 5th row! Being that close for the first time brought a whole new dimension to the Rod experience. It was a completely different show. You could see the interaction between Rod, the fans, and the band to a degree that you just can't see from the upper levels. The energy Rod exuded and generated took my breath away. He made it look effortless but more importantly, he was enjoying himself. He went out of his way to make the show personal for those lucky few that he sang to, pointed at, bowed to or gave a soccer ball to. And to be there with a bunch of people you know and who are feeling what you are feeling made it even more intense. If that wasn't enough, afterwards we were invited by a very special Smiler member, who is now the USA secretary, to go over to the hotel where the band was staying. I couldn't believe what I was hearing. Of course, we went, and Rita went out of her way to introduce me to several of the band members. I will never forget that! Talk about a dream come true! Initially, I didn't want to do or say anything to bother them, but Rita felt that it was OK and off we went. That whole night was like slow motion and for days afterward I kept thinking 'Did that really happen?'

That concert in Pittsburgh was the start of a whole new level of my Rod experience. A group of us went back to NYC again to see Rod in Madison Square Garden. I couldn't even comprehend what it would be like to see Rod up close in a venue the size of the MSG. What a great time we had getting ready for the concert then I heard the bad news. I remember getting out of the shower and my friends looking pale saying that Rod had canceled due to throat problems. I thought it was a bad joke, but it was true. We cried. All the money we spent, all the anticipation! We were devastated. What could we do? We had dinner at Kennedy's and a few of the band members were there who were kind enough to give us autographs and took pictures with us. Then we heard that some of the band might be playing and singing at a place called Le Bar Bat, right near Kennedy's as a former guitar player from Rod's band was in town. A few of us went and we were not disappointed! The guys played and sang until the place closed up. I was mesmerized listening. It was one thing to hear them singing backup vocals with Rod, but to hear them sing by themselves was incredible. They were so kind to talk to us. It meant so much to me that these guys would be so down to earth to take time to make us feel special. I will never forget that.

I got sick in NYC, with what I thought was a cold but no matter, the Cleveland and Cincinnati concerts were only a few days away. We had 3rd row seats that night and, believe it or not, my mother was coming to that concert! Both of us had our first Rod Moments at that show! I had brought a sign that said 'Rod, we missed you in MSG.' During 'Maggie May' he read it, smiled, bowed to me and pointed to his throat! I was so stunned, I had to sit down a minute, which was probably the only minute I have ever voluntarily sat at a Rod concert. Rod came down off the stage once, too, and grabbed my hand as he went by. I screamed to my mother that he grabbed my hand and she said, very proudly, that he had grabbed hers, too! Back when I was listening to Rod in my room as a teen, I never in a million years would have thought that I would be sharing a Rod Moment with my mom! How special that was to me! I had also brought another sign with me for the band that said 'You were dynamite at Le Bar Bat.' To my delight, one of the guys, Dee, saw it, got the attention of another band member, Freddie, and both read it. They smiled and Dee nodded his head and tapped his finger on his temple as if to say, 'Yes, I remember you.' Again, another first that is etched in my mind forever. The following night was Cincinnati. A friend of mine and I had taken off work and made the three hour drive to that venue. Once again at will call we picked up our tickets. I didn't even look at the tickets, but the girl behind the counter looked at me and said that they were pretty good seats. They said row 'A' but I couldn't let myself think they were front row. We made our way down to the floor and sure enough, front row center!! I cried. It was an awesome experience. I had slipped down to the rail before, but this was the first time I was supposed to be there! I had plenty of Rod Moments that night and was so high on adrenaline I had no trouble making the three hour trip back to Cleveland. I look back now and wonder how I even survived. I was still sick and went to the doctor who told me that I had pneumonia!

The last couple of years have been phenomenal for me. Because of a situation out of our immediate control, the ticket situation has become a little more difficult, but I have been blessed enough to have had seats in the first few rows. It has been a thrill to have been able to attend shows, near and far with my Rod friends. The circumstances and road trips have given us all memories that we will cherish forever. Who else but my Rod friends would walk into FAO Schwartz in NYC and make Rod necklaces out of alphabet letters and soccer ball beads? Who else would find a street artist in Central Park and have him come to the hotel to do chalk sketches of Rod? Who else would drive to

Indianapolis and sit in 90 plus degree heat and sun holding our places at the rail waiting for a free Rod concert? Who else would play an entire Rod CD on a juke box in a little local bar and drive out all the 'regulars?' Who else would go shopping with you and stop to look at everything leopard print and tartan? And who else would think to get me a graduation present of a personally autographed tour book? Yes, a few of my friends online knew that I did not have anything autographed by Rod and they arranged to get a tour book to the UK Smiler secretary who gave it to Rod and had him sign it 'Congratulations, Janice - Rod Stewart.' That meant more to me than words can describe.

My sister and I had the privilege of going to the UK in December 1998 to see 5 concerts, 2 in Glasgow, Scotland and 3 in London, England. In learning about Rod, it doesn't take long to discover how important his Scottish heritage is to him and I couldn't think of a better place than Scotland to share a few hours with him! I had been thinking about seeing some shows over there for years, but never really thought it would happen. Well, my other Rod Angel, the Smiler UK secretary, Marilyn, made sure Smiler members had tickets and even took care of making hotel reservations for us, even though she had never met us in person before. Marilyn had every detail worked out and even called our room from England to make sure we had arrived safely. I can only say that the next two days were the most incredible of my life. We met Marilyn the next day who introduced us to fans from the UK. They made us feel so welcome and once again, it was like we had known each other for years. As the concerts were general admission, Marilyn had arranged for Smiler members to go in first to ensure a spot at the rail. We were in the front row in Glasgow, Scotland. Quite a far cry from the upper level seats I had grown accustomed to just a few years ago! It was an emotional moment for me, to say the least. I had tears in my eyes as the show started. There's something magical about the fans over there. I looked around at a sea of tartan and saw every person standing, cheering and singing like nothing I had ever heard in the USA. At times, the crowd seemed louder than Rod himself and even Rod seemed humbled by the response he was getting. It was the sweetest moment to see the look on his face. I was awestruck. It was refreshing to hear Rod sing 'Sailing' as the encore. The next night was even more special. Once again at the rail, we were watching as Rod was kicking out soccer balls. To my utter amazement, Rod stood in front of me and read a sign that I had brought saying that I had come from Cleveland for a soccer ball. He motioned for a soccer ball to be thrown out to him. He caught it and handed it directly to me! I can't even describe what those few seconds were like for me. It could not possibly get any better than that. A soccer ball from Rod in Glasgow. After the shows it was wonderful to see the band again and hear from them how powerful it was even for them to look out at the crowd and see that reaction. You have to actually experience it for the full affect. We moved on to London and met the rest of the USA fans that had also come over for the shows. Those three shows were incredible, but those two Glasgow concerts hold a special place in my heart. My two most recent memories were from a concert in Erie, PA, my hometown, in April 1999 and from a trip to Atlantic City in June 1999. Rod was playing smaller venues and I was excited that Rod was playing in Erie, PA. My mother stood in line at a TicketMaster and bought tickets for my father and her. I opted to try to get better tickets through other channels. It didn't work and as a last resort, tried for late release tickets the day of the show. It could have only been a miracle, but two second row seats were available. When we got inside, no one was in the front row seats right in front of us so we moved up. There I was, front row in my hometown! My mom and dad had great seats in the first level and were thrilled some of the signs projected onto the big screen as the camera guy focused in on them a few times. I had many Rod Moments during that show, but was thrilled when Rod ran over to me and handed me another soccer ball!! How ironic. My first soccer ball was given to me in Glasgow, a place that meant a lot to him, and then the second one given to me in Erie, my hometown, a place that meant a lot to me. Later that summer, in June, I had the opportunity to go to Atlantic City for two shows. I had a fantastic time with my Rod Angels who I roomed with. I was able to be a part of some wonderful conversations with them and several of Rod's band members and can't thank them enough for the kindness they showed me. It still astonishes me every time I have the opportunity to be with these people on that level. It really wasn't all that long ago that I was staring at the stage through binoculars wondering how in the world I could get closer. Now look what's happened to me. It's been nothing short of miraculous, divine intervention and a little help from my Rod Angels, to be sure.

To try to sum it all up, my Rod experiences over the last two decades has been life changing. Yes, I have gone to measures that some may think is extreme, but I am not a 'groupie,' have no criminal record, and am not a stalker or a psycho hiding out in dressing rooms and following tour buses and limos. I'm a regular person. I have a master's degree in education, a full-time job and am a home owner. I have other friends and interests that are not at all Rod related. I have never met Rod. Rod Stewart is simply a very dear part of my life. I have been fortunate enough to have developed friendships as a result and have been privileged to interact with individuals close to Rod. I have the utmost respect for these individuals and would never do anything to break that bond. The Rod experience is equally about getting together with my friends as it is about the actual concert itself. Of course, one day I would love to thank Rod in person for all the happiness his music has brought into my life. So far that hasn't happened, but that's OK. Maybe one day it will."

- Janice Bernhard

* * *

Reflections on Rod Stewart by a 'Rod' Lookalike from Texas

"Rod Stewart means different things to different people. As for myself, Rod Stewart changed my life. It all started on Halloween afternoon 1991. I had been trying to figure out what I was going to wear to a huge Halloween Bash that night when all of a sudden I was drawn to an MTV video that was playing. It was the Rod Stewart video of 'My Heart Can't Tell You' in which Rod is wearing a T-shirt and jeans at the end of the video. It was like divine inspiration (after all I owned a white T-shirt and torn blue jeans). I decided to attend this party as 'Rod Stewart.'

Although I had dark brown hair at the time, I knew it would work because all the girls I knew in college called me 'Rod' because of my features. So I attempted to dress as Rod. I sprayed a whole can of $4.00 bleach blonde hairspray dye and partied the night away with my hair in it's chaotic and 100% flammable state.

It was a night that seemed meant to be because aside from causing a commotion. I won. the costume contest and got 'discovered' by a local talent agency that deals with celebrity lookalikes and impersonators. Needless to say, my life hasn't been the same since.

To make a truly longer story shorter....It took almost 4 years for this agent to convince me to give it a shot. Since then I've done many 'appearances' and performed many a 'Rod' tribute show, including one event in front of 18,500 people and winning many more contests. Yes, this 'Rod lookalike' gig has given me many opportunities to have good times, enjoy great music and meet great people including my wife and some of Rod's band members.

My wife was attracted to me because she was a big Rod Steward fan. Ironically, she would pass for Rachel Hunter. Unfortunately, and even more ironical we separated in 1999, just like Rod and Rachel.

On a more positive note, one of my most memorable 'Rod' moments was after a Rod concert in San Antonio, Texas in 1996 when I got to meet Freddie, Dee and Lamont, Rod's backup singers. We caused a big commotion walking on the San Antoino Riverwalk as I showed them around. They got a kick out of it.

In 1999, San Antoino once again, Dee and some Rod crew members caught one of my 'tribute' shows and had a blast with it even helping me do a little 'Hot Legs.' The stories can go on and on.

As you can see, Rod Stewart, the rock star, sex symbol or great songwriter, whatever he is to others, means a great deal to me. I was always aware of him and liked his songs while I was growing up. I tried to learn 'You're In My Heart' on my guitar when I was in the seventh grade....but now I'm a huge fan who loves to promote him the way I get to....some guys have all the luck, right!?"

- Victor Rodriguez

Rod with wife, Alana Hamilton.

* * *

"I've been a Rod fan since 1971, and have been to 69 concerts from Sat. July 1, 1972 to Sun. June 27, 1999 and have met him three times.

On Wed. May 2, 1973 I went to see The Faces concert in Boston. Rod wore a blue glitter tank top, feather boa around his waist and yellow satin slacks.

After the concert I went to the hotel where I knew the band was staying and was fortunate enough to go to the party afterwards.

I was waiting to use the bathroom, standing alone near the front of the room, when in walked Rod, looked over at me and headed into the party with all the rest. I couldn't believe it. All The Faces were now there, except Ronnie Lane.

As the night went on Rod was sitting in a corner chair with a large group of girls kneeling around him. I was drinking a bottle of Portuguese wine and decided to go over and ask him to sign it, after I had finished it. Even though I felt funny, I had to go over, I'd never get this chance again.

Walking over, I asked Rod if he would mind signing the empty bottle. He looked up curiously, the girls all hissed at me and told me to get lost. I felt badly and started to walk away. The next thing, Rod snapped his fingers loudly and motioned for me to return. He said to give him the bottle, I did, he signed it, passed it back to me and said, 'Hey kid, have a good time, relax and enjoy the party.'

Shortly after that with another snap of his fingers he was gone, with his blonde for the evening. This happened to me when I was sixteen years old, no one at school ever believed me. I have so many great memories over the years, of the music and concerts, but that night was something else. I still have the wine bottle."

- Alan Jackson

* * *

Alan Jackson.

Rachel Hunter, Rod Stewart and
Terrance Trent D'Arby.

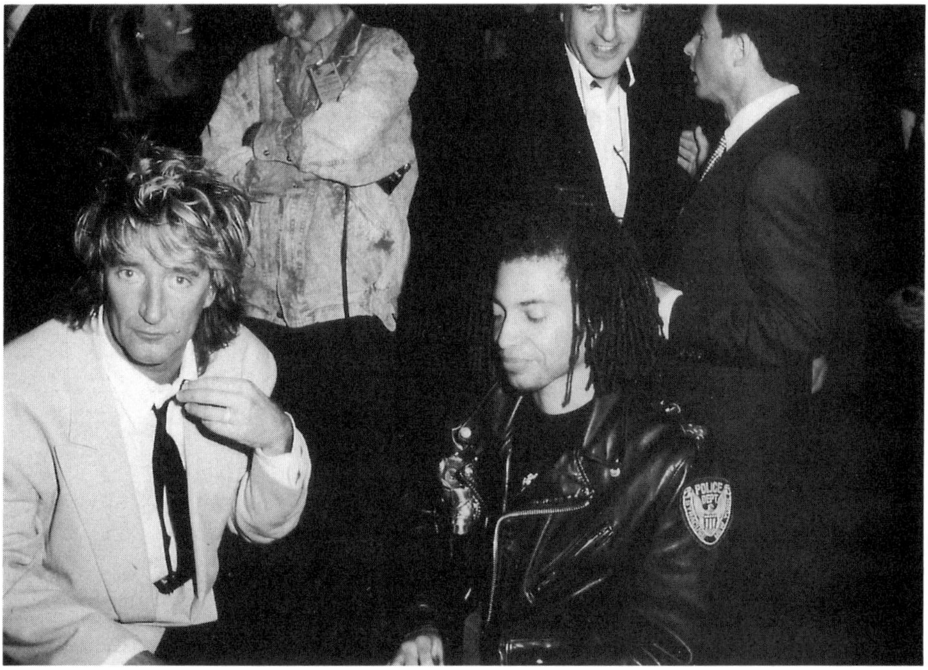
POLICE
DEPT

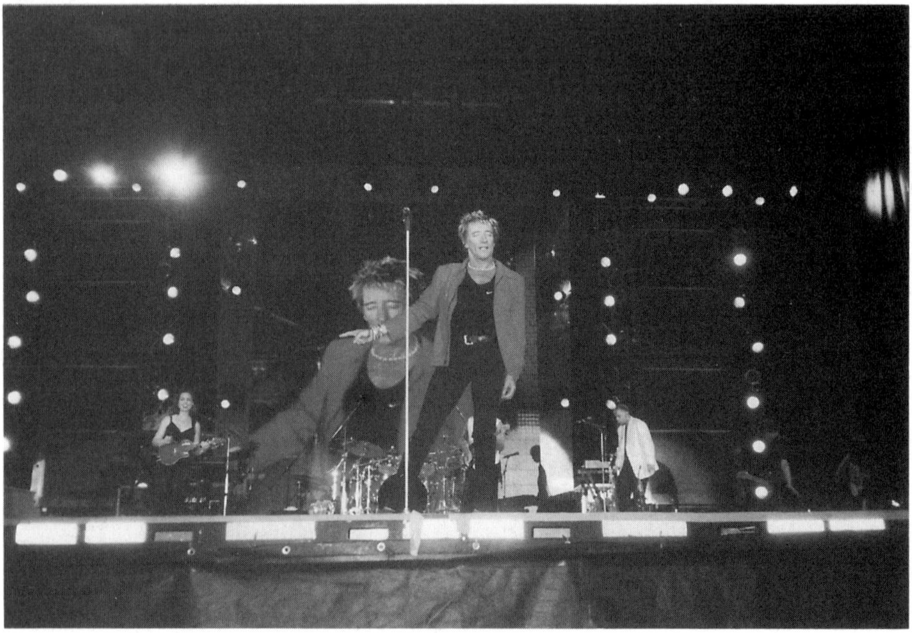

87

Fan's Concert Reviews and Stories

The following two concert reviews and stories are by Rod Stewart fan, Mike Gregor.

"Raleigh, NC - Rod Stewart and the band jumped up on stage on this hot and steamy night at the Alltel Pavilion at Walnut Creek for another sing-a-long of the Rock n' Roll legend's countless classic songs. The musicians, just coming off a month long hiatus, seemed rested and ready to get it going again.

Rod opened with 'Tonight I'm Yours,' and indeed he was, as he thrilled the audience, both young and old, with all the hits. The crowd was entertained for more than two hours as Rod found time to wipe the sweat from his brow, especially after performing the cut 'Rocks,' which is on the latest recording 'When We Were The New Boys.' Later, Rod stood silent while the sea of fans gave something back to the performer by singing the lyrics of the hit 'Tonight's The Night,' to him word for word.

The highlight of this evening came during the classic hit 'You're In My Heart,' when nearing the end of the song, a group of obviously Rod's biggest fans, waved a gift high in the air toward the stage from their front and center seating. Rod reached out and accepted the gift, and after scanning over the framed collection of CELTIC players' trading cards he requested a camera shot of the work. While it was displayed on the several large projection screens so the entire audience could see, the performer thanked these fans for the wonderful gift, a collector's item of his favorite team from Scotland. Rod demonstrated his sincere appreciation shortly thereafter as he tossed one of the coveted autographed soccer balls to them.

Later in the show, while the band performed the Sam Cooke classic 'Having A Party,' a gigantic soccer ball hanging high above the crowd opened up and dropped hundreds of white balloons to the waiting fans. The concert saw an encore, the ageless hit 'Maggie May,' just before Rod and his band waved farewell to the crowd and disappeared as the curtain fell in front of the stage.

Reports from the local airport shortly after the show commented that Rod boarded his private jet, wearing a big smile and carrying the framed set of CELTIC cards in hand."

* * *

"Indianapolis, IN - The lightning flashed across the evening sky as a sign of the electricity that would soon climb up on the temporary stage over North Street. Moments earlier while a light rain fell, the group Kool & the Gang somehow subdued the group who had been anxiously waiting since daybreak for the main act.

As the sun crept over the horizon on Saturday morning, a group of strangers gathered in the grass of the American Legion Mall in downtown Indianapolis. The meeting place was no coincidence for these peo-

Rod with the framed Celtic cards that was given to him.

The crew of Rod fans ready to give Rod
the framed Celtic cards.

Getting ready to go to the concert to give Rod the framed Celtic cards.

ple, but rather a well planned occasion to come together for the free concert in downtown featuring Kool & the Gang and Rod Stewart. They had travelled from several different states including Florida, Georgia, Ohio and West Virginia, not to miss this show. As they watched the downtown street being transformed into a massive stage, they exchanged memories of past shows and experiences surrounding the Scottish rock star.

The group of about twenty, had only one thing in common prior to this day, and that was their infatuation for the 54 year old performer who is but a living example of one of his biggest hits, 'Forever Young.' Through the power of the internet, their worlds would be brought together for this occasion as the complete strangers spent the long day together. Any on-lookers would have argued that the group was most certainly family and were involved in some sort of reunion.

Rod the Mod Stewart hit the stage with an explosion unmatched by the passing storm as he opened up the concert with 'Tonight I'm Yours.' It set the stage for the night, as he went on to perform many hits from his past as well as 'Rocks,' one of his latest recordings. Later, Rod turned the evening into a tribute of sorts to his biggest musical influence, the legendary Sam Cooke. Rod performed 'Having A Party' and 'Cupid' before returning for an encore of 'Maggie May.'

The crowd of 75,000 was loud, and at times out of control as the general admission event caused many to push and shove while attempting to reach the front of the crowd. Through it all, the faithful pact of true fans got what they came for, as the security crew knew them all well from the long day and made certain they maintained their place front and center of the stage. Even the band recognized the group from several earlier gigs they had played since late February.

Nearing the end of the performance, a fireworks display lit up the sky to the right of the stage, which appeared to be only a flicker in the night compared to the amount of energy that was showered over the crowd from center stage. Rod was spectacular this night, as he was seemingly delighted to play before a crowd of this size for the first time in several years. Rod touched the hearts and souls of all in attendance with the internal fire he holds for his music.

For the newly made friends the following day was bittersweet as it meant goodbye to one another. As each drove away, they all realized, just as they would the music from 'Mr. Stewart,' the time spent together here in Indianapolis would be kept alive in their hearts forever."

* * *

The following three concert reviews and stories are from Rod Stewart fan, Lynn Proctor.

"We left early Wednesday morning for KY. We got there only to discover I had left our tickets in WV. How stupid could I be? We had to make a decision, drive 3 hours back home and then 3 hours back again, or buy new tickets. We decided to buy new tickets. We got 21st row on the floor which was actually better than our old tickets. I wanted to get closer if possible so when we got to Freedom Hall we talked to a couple of scalpers. Nothing better, then someone approached me and said, 'Are you the one?' (I'm still not sure where that came from), but I glanced at him and said, 'What?' He asked, 'Do you want a ticket?' My husband thought, OK maybe we can get a good ticket. So he came over and said, 'Where is the seat?' The guy replied, 'It doesn't matter, it is free.' And he then gave me a 13th row ticket. I, idiot that I am, did not even recognize him! But my husband did! It was Carmine Rojas!! And I had no camera! Mitch, my husband, told him that we had seen them Sunday night and he asked, 'Any good?' Mitch told him it was great! He said thanks and we thanked him for the ticket and he went back inside.

When we were inside I got to meet a very nice guy that sat next to me. His name was Dan and he told me about growing up with Carmine and playing in a band together in Dan's basement. His wife could not make the show so he had told Carmine to give the other ticket away. I told him I was very grateful! Dan also told me that he had been backstage when Rod got there at 8:25 and that Rod had been upset because his plane had been late. At 8:35 Rod came out on stage. He was tired and it showed and the first few songs were a little shaky. Then he broke into 'Infatuation' and I was amazed. I wondered where all the energy had come from all of a sudden. He was playing the crowd and they were loving it! It just got better and better.

When Rod sang 'You're In My Heart' there was video of him and Liam on the screen playing soccer. Rod started having trouble getting through the song and turned his back to the audience to sing. His voice was cracking and my heart was breaking! When he was done he said, 'That one is a bit too emotional. Let's pick it up.' He then went into a fast song. He took gifts, signed an autograph, kicked soccer balls, winked at the girls in the front row and shook hands with the guys. At one point he went down in the audience, put his back to the lower balcony and three women leaned over, put their arms around him and were rubbing his chest while he sang! (I need a cold shower just thinking about it!). We were having so much fun. People came down from the upper levels to fill the aisles and dance. Dan turned to me and said,

'This is awesome!' I had to agree! Rod also sang 'Do Ya Think I'm Sexy?' and the crowd went wild! He also sang 'Tonight's The Night' and the audience sang a couple of verses alone. He loved it! He commented that he had not sang those two songs in a while and how much fun it was. He finally left the stage and, of course, came back to sing 'Maggie.' Then he left again. The crowd was screaming and stomping and yelling for more. They did not turn the lights on or close the curtain so we stayed.

Sure enough, he came back! He said that we could feel free to leave because they were just going to rehearse! I wasn't going anywhere! He sang a song I had never heard. I think it was an old song, I'm not sure. Then he said, 'We are going to do it again. I told you this was a rehearsal.' We were all standing on our seats and screaming. The floor was crowded with people who had come down from the upper seats. When they finished the song a second time Rod said, 'That's all. Thanks for staying. I love to have an audience when I rehearse. Now we are going to the bar!' And he was gone! What an awesome show! It was two hours long."

* * *

"This story starts with meeting a real friend online. We talked for weeks and then decided that he would try to come to Charleston, WV, where I live, to see Rod with me. I already had tickets, but now we had to find some for him and his date, that he also met online. I tried several different places for good tickets but to no avail. Then, on March 10th I had an email from Molly McLaren at Stiefel Entertainment telling me I had won tickets to the Charleston show. Wow, a prayer answered. My friends, Mike and Tami, were going to be in Greensboro, NC the night before the Charleston show to see Rod there. So, they decided to drive to

Charleston the next day. We met at 4:00 pm and had a nice dinner. They were everything I had hoped they would be, true Rod fans and really great people! Mike had even made me a Rod shirt!After dinner we went to the Civic Center to pick up the tickets I won, there was a mix up at the window and it was 8:10 pm before we got the tickets. We were getting really nervous! Then when everything was worked out we ended up with 2nd row center! That left Mike and Tami with 5th row center. We were all thrilled! Then to make it even better, no one was in the seat in front of me so I climbed over and there I was FRONT ROW CENTER! When Rod came out on stage I thought I would die, he was so close! I wore a Celtic jersey for him. After the second song he looked at me and said, 'I like your shirt.' I was in heaven! He had noticed me! The show was great, he sounded great and looked even better!

When they brought a piano out on stage and Rod walked over to it he looked at me again and pointed to my shirt and winked. He noticed me again! Then he sang 'You're In My Heart.' When he sang the words, 'You're Celtic United,' he pointed at me again! I was so glad I had worn that shirt! I couldn't take my eyes off him the whole show. I know the band was great and Rod at times wanted the crowd to acknowledge the band, but all I saw was Rod! At one point in the show security was going to throw a lady out, Rod was singing 'Rhythm of My Heart.' He actually stopped the show, leaned down and took the woman's hand and asked her what was going on. She told him she was being thrown out and he said, 'No you are not!' and told security to leave her alone. Then he started the song from the beginning.

When the time came for 'Cut Across Shorty' I was at the stage only a few feet from Rod, he looked at me again and smiled. I think he really liked my shirt! All too soon the show was ending. I had really hoped to get a soccer ball this time, but at least Rod had talked to me, winked at me and smiled at me. What more could a woman want in this life? Well, I got it! When he finished the last song he came over to me, took off his hat and handed it down. Everyone around me was trying to grab it so he pulled it back, shook his head, pointed to me, knelt down and handed me his hat !!! I have never been so happy! After the show my new friends and my husband and I went to have coffee. We talked about the show and about Rod and had a great time. They are on their way back home now and I miss them already. Thanks to the Internet, Cyber Club and most of all the Love of my life, Rod Stewart for the Night of my life !!"

* * *

"I arrived in Burgettstown, PA with my six-year-old daughter, Rachel, ready to rock! I met up with some friends I had met on Saturday. We went down and coped out our seats. They had front row and I had second, but there were no seats in front of me. Cheryl's three-year-old son, Andrew, wanted some popcorn so we went to get it and who do we see? Freddie White! He was also buying pop corn. We talked to me for a few minutes and then here came Lamont Van Hook. We got to talk to both of them for a while and got autographs and a couple of pictures with them. Right before they left Lamont said, 'Wait! I want my picture taken with this little lady.' And he leaned down and put his arms around my daughter and put his face next to hers. It is a wonderful picture. I got the chance to tell Lamont that I was in the group of fans that gave the framed Celtic cards in Raleigh and he said, 'Oh yeah! Rod was really bragging on that....he loved it!' What a thing to hear!!

We went back to our seats and saw some new friends from Indy and met a couple more Internet friends in person. Then Tracey told me that another friend was waiting for me outside the gates. I went and got her and found that she had bought a seat...FRONT ROW CENTER!! She opted to trade seats with a new friend and sit next to me, but with the first beat of music we stood up and moved to the gate, so there we were....FRONT ROW AGAIN!! And what a show! I believe Rod gets better and better with each show I see. Before the curtain was raised we could see under it and see Rod's purple shoes jumping around. That just added to the excitement!

The front row was once again lined with True fans...and that's the way it should be. My young daughter was in awe. She has heard Rod's music and seen pictures all her life. She even has Rod posters in her room and is named after Rachel Hunter. But as we all know...Nothing compares to seeing Rod in person! She had brought a soccer beanie baby bear to give to Rod. She held it up every time he would come near, but it took forever for him to take it from her. Finally, the moment came when he did and a loud cheer erupted from the crowd around us. I got a picture of Rod actually taking the beanie baby from Rachel's hand....something I will cherish forever! (See photo on page 53). He then got a soccer ball and tossed it to her. And she caught it herself! Just as Rod was starting to walk away he caught site of Rachel's shirt so he read it. It said, 'Mom loves Rod so she named me Rachel.' He smiled at that and pointed at her.

At one point in the show Rod accepted a gift from a lady. It was a book of Sam Cooke's life. He showed it to all of us and said, 'I shall read it tonight.' I know she was thrilled! During 'Having A Party' Rod invited a lady personally to come on stage. I got her picture and she looks really happy! Then other fans started getting on stage. Cheryl was over the barrier in a heart beat! I got stopped by the camera guy (but, of

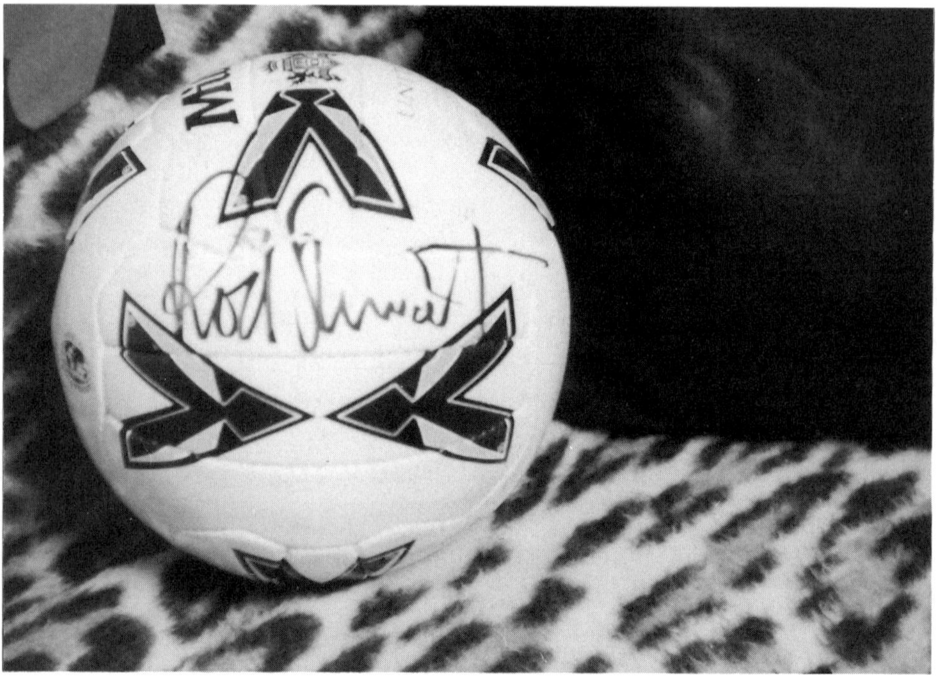

course, we all knew I would not get close enough to touch him!). Cheryl got to dance with her arm around him and his around her! LUCKY HER!! When the balloons dropped Rachel had a ball....she came home with 6 balloons stamped with ROD STEWART!

Rod really seemed to be having fun. He even told us to look at the beautiful sunset. Like good little fans we all turned and looked when Rod told us to, but I quickly looked back at him. I didn't want to miss a minute of looking at him! I again Loved his version of 'Cupid.' He commented a couple of times on the audience and how much he was enjoying himself. The encore came. Always such a sad time for me. I never wanted it to end. Seems neither did Rod on this night. After 'Maggie Mae' he said, 'OK, that was the end of the show. Feel free to go home, but we are going to rehearse for Glasgow. We are going to rehearse some that we do there, but not here!' And he proceeded to sing 'Baby Jane.' Then it was over! I'd give ANYTHING to be in Glasgow!! Another awesome show over and great memories for me."

* * *

The following story is from Rod Stewart fan Debbie Fumagalli. Debbie has MS and she had a nice encounter with Rod at a taping of the Oprah Winfrey show.

"I've been a huge fan of Rod Stewart since I've been old enough to appreciate music. I am now 37 years old. I always admired the lyrics of his songs, I love how he always has a story to tell in his music - brilliant song writing. Then I saw him perform and I couldn't believe his energy. From the first moment, I was hooked. To hear a concert is one thing. To feel it is quite another. Over the years, I have lost count as to how many times I've seen him perform.

A highlight came for me when I heard he was to be at a CD signing at a record store here in Chicago. At the time I was acquainted with one of Oprah Winfrey's camera men who told me Rod was scheduled to tape a show. That was all the information I needed. I reserved two seats in her studio audience, but was told the show was overbooked. I would receive a call back from the studio if I would be able to get in. They asked me how long I'd been a fan and what my favorite song was. I guess I passed because they phoned me back and told me to be at the studio the next day.

The following day my husband and I were in route to Harpo studios where the show would be taped. After we checked through security we took a seat outside the stage doors. You could hear Rod rehearsing. Over the intercom we were told this taping was going to take longer than anticipated, the studio would provide lunch, stay patient, eat and they would call upon us when it came time for seating. All this because Rod wanted to rehearse.

I have MS and I use a cane to help me walk. When the studio allowed us in finally, we luckily took seats directly in front of Oprah's stage. Row 2. The studio filled and we were all waiting when the woman in front of me turned around and asked me if I would trade seats with her. As she put it, she didn't want Rod to notice her. Of course, I leaped from my chair and traded seats. Now I was directly front and center stage. My husband was seated behind me. It all happened so fast. Oprah was announced, she walked out and stopped directly in front of me. She opened the show and introduced Rod. He walked out and grabbed Oprah by the hand and they moved to the piano, and begun singing medleys. The studio audience went crazy. Even Oprah was surprised, you clearly see this by her reaction. Let's talk energy again. You couldn't believe it. The show went on. Oprah went ahead with her interview with Rod and it was clear that she didn't know a whole lot about him. She was totally stunned how the audience reacted to his presence. He sang 'If We Fall In Love Tonight,' answered some questions, interacted with the audience and before you knew it, the show was over. The studio began to empty. We stayed put because we were to hook up with my friend (the camera man). He was going to give us a tour of Harpo Studios. Ten to fifteen minutes passed. I never thought Rod would still be back stage. When we headed behind the scenes, to my absolute astonishment he was just standing there along with the woman I had traded seats with. I learned later this was Anne Challis, his manager. I had a picture in my purse I had taken of him months before and had enlarged it to a 5 x 7...just in case! The words just came out of my mouth, 'Rod would you sign a picture for me?' 'Sure,' he said. 'Did something to your leg, did you?' he asked. 'I have MS,' I replied. 'Really,' he stated, 'My sister had MS.' I knew his mom suffered from this disease, but I never heard about his sister. I also knew his friend and bandmate Ronnie Lane had MS and recently died. Anyway, I began my frantic search through my purse for the picture and I drop my cane. (I think) I acted as calm as ever when really I was ready to drop. He bent down, picked up my cane and held it until I got myself together. I finally got the picture out and handed it to him and he handed me back my cane. He asked where I had taken this picture as he signed his name across it. Then he turned to Anne and asked for a promo photo. She took out a 8 x 10 Warner Brothers black & white picture from her case. He asked my name, wrote it on the picture and signed his name again. He handed it to me and thanked me for my support. Then I asked him where he got the name for a Faces album, 'A Nod Is As Good As A Wink To A

Blind Horse.' Why I asked this question, I have no idea? He said he couldn't take credit for that, it was an old English verse. The entire time Oprah was standing there waiting. I thanked Rod and turned to my husband with disbelief and astonishment. When I got outside I screamed. To this day, I have difficulty believing this all happened. If I didn't have the tape of the show, I would still be questioning my luck. Because I'm directly in front, I am highly visible. In fact, you know how Oprah opens her show everyday showing audience members. Well, my husband and I made it on her show opener for the next year. Every morning we were shown laughing. (Our kids loved it!) The reason we were laughing is because Rod was quoted as saying, referring to his wife Rachel, he had found the girl of his dreams wouldn't be putting his banana in anyone else's fruit bowl! What a riot.

A few months after the taping my husband and I were front row to yet another Rod concert in Chicago. I was on my scooter when he came on stage, when he saw us he waved. As fast as I could get my body to move, I got up and propped myself against an amp. When he kicked out soccer balls he walked over, smiled and tossed me a ball. I couldn't believe I caught it. The ball is autographed, and any true fan would know what a treasure I have - personally hand delivered nonetheless. I wondered if he remembered us, it seemed as if he did. You know, I always thought that to meet Rod Stewart, he would be an arrogant jerk. The exact opposite was true. He was kind, compassionate and friendly. It makes me admire him more remembering how personable he was to me."

* * *

Football man.

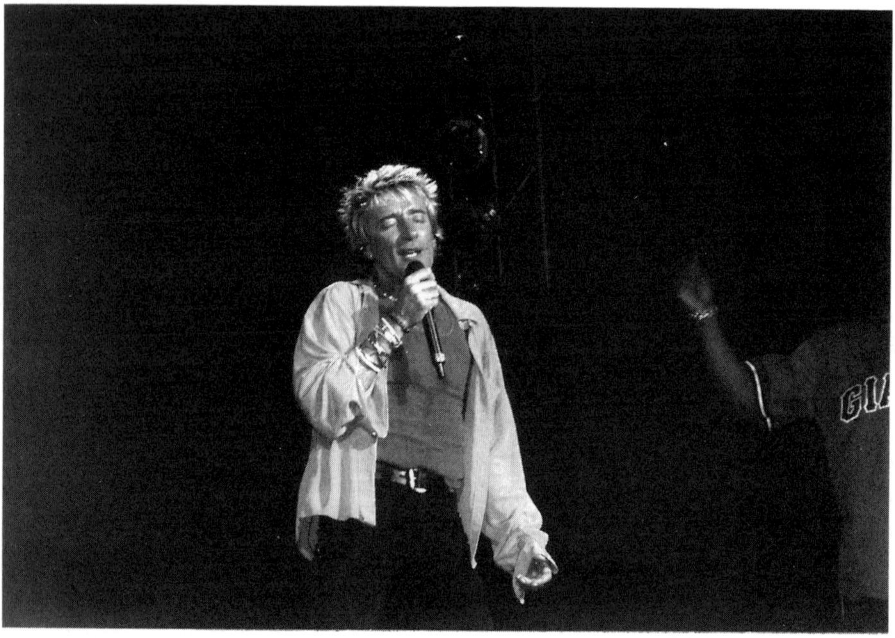

107

The following, amusing story of some Rod Encounters is from Marcy Braunstein.

"I had plenty of photos of Rod Stewart from the many concerts I'd been to, and also from a few lucky encounters I had had with him when he was coming and going in lobbies of hotels. I shook his hand back in 1985, handed him several gifts from the audience at a number of shows which resulted in Rod presenting me with a signed soccer ball. I got his autograph at 4:00 am in the lobby of the Bally's Grand Hotel during one of those encounters! I even bumped into him (literally) one time backstage, and was so stunned I couldn't even open my mouth to say anything, which is another story all in itself. But my lifelong dream was to have my picture taken with the man, whose international fan club, Smiler, I was a card-carrying member of. This was the man for whom I've traveled many miles to see (twice to England) over the years and to whom I've devoted an entire room in my house with a wide range of memorabilia, affectionately referred to as my 'Rod Room.'

Two previous attempts at a picture with him had failed. The first time was in a hotel lobby before a concert in Philadelphia, while with a friend who was also a fan. I had waited hours there and finally spotted him right before he got on the elevator and I asked him if I could take a picture with him. Unfortunately for me, in the excitement, my friend stepped into the picture instead of me. Another time was when Rod came through the lobby of a hotel in Cleveland and again, in the excitement, I ended up with a beautiful picture of another friend of mine with Rod, and my arm!

It was midway through what was probably my

29th, or 30th show this tour and here we were, my husband and I, front row center at the Taj Mahal in Atlantic City. As usual, I had a number of signs in tow that I made to hold up during my favorite songs. I had my green and white Celtic scarf that I waved during my very favorite song 'You're In My Heart,' also a laminated, yet still very worn 'Lost In You Since '72' sign for what else, but during the 80's song 'Lost In You' and a tartan scarf for the old Faces hit 'Stay With Me.' I'd even made this one for his new album 'Rod, you look and sound as good as When You Were The New Boys.' Most times, Rod would acknowledge my efforts with a nod of the head, a smile or sometimes he would even throw a kiss my way, which would send me over the top. I certainly agree with a fellow fan club member , who wrote online, that you don't really see Rod at a concert unless he also sees you.

It was getting late in the tour and I was really determined to catch his attention and to do everything right this time, so I took a slightly different approach. I made a sign for my dear husband to hold up which read, 'Hey Rod, my wife has been nagging me for 20 years to have her picture taken with you. C'mon Rod, get her off my back!' Truer words have never been written, as I really had enlisted my very patient husband, Dave, in my mission to get that long awaited picture.

When Rod started to sing Sam Cooke's 'Twisting The Night Away,' a song during which I'd previously seen Rod welcome fans on stage, I motioned for Dave to hold up that large, bright neon, green sign I'd made. Rod was singing, dancing and strutting and started to head toward the middle of the stage. My husband was successful by holding the sign high enough for one of Rod's back-up singers, Lamont Van Hook, to read it. Lamont tugged on Rod's shirt sleeve and pointed to the sign. Rod stopped in his tracks, read

Marcy Braunstein, her sign and Rod.

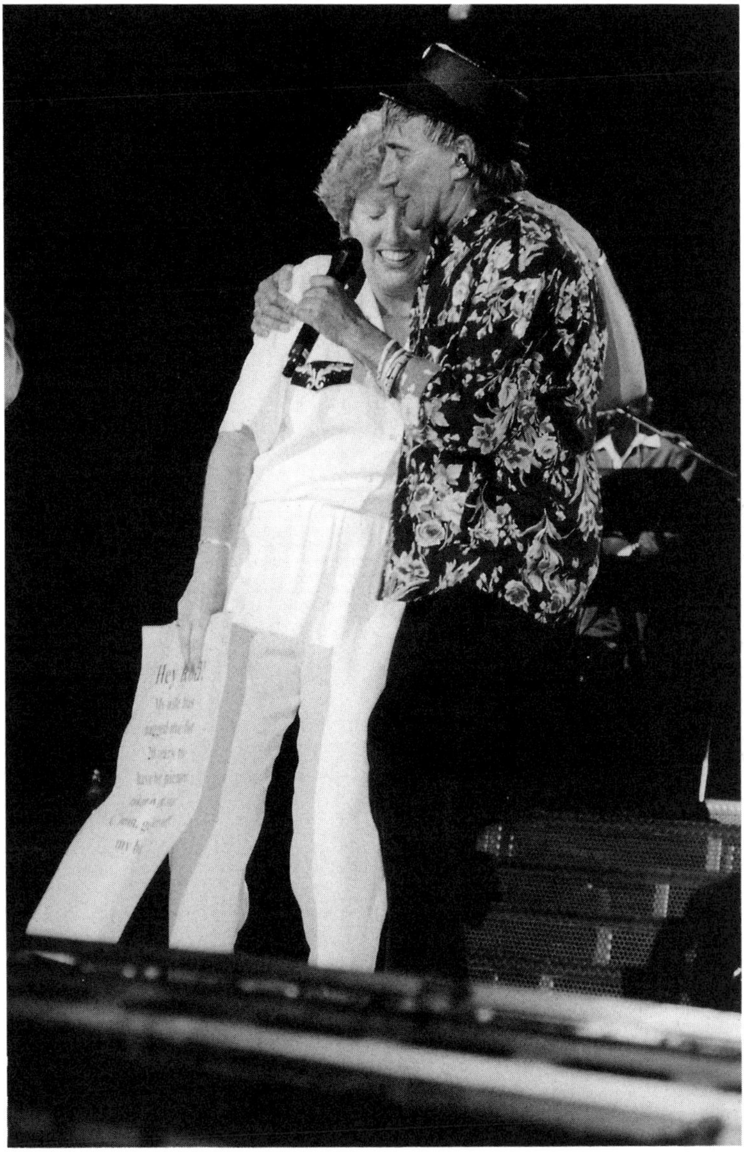

the sign, looked down at Dave and then at the anxious expression on my face and said the words that I can still hear, 'Come on up!'

Rod motioned for security to help me up on the stage. I don't know how I did it, but I literally jumped over the barricade that protected the stage from the audience and somehow I was lifted up over the speakers and other equipment and onto the stage. Rod put his arm around me and I immediately hugged him and I just couldn't stop saying, 'Oh Rod, thank you!' He asked Dave to give our camera to security and he posed with me for the picture. He motioned for Dave to hand the sign up to me so the audience could read it. We danced together during the entire song, he even gave me the microphone at one point. I couldn't believe I was actually dancing and singing with Rod Stewart! When the song was over, I hugged him one final time and thanked him again for what would be my most memorable experience. Security helped me down the steps from what I considered 'heaven.' When I got back to my seat, Rod came over to where my husband and I were standing and said, 'She won't be nagging you anymore, will she?' Rod was right about that, because I hugged and kissed my wonderful husband and will be eternally grateful to him for helping me finally have my dream come true.

Since I couldn't wait any longer to see the picture of Rod and myself on the stage together, my husband and I stopped at a one-hour photo shop the next morning on our way to the next show (in Washington D.C.) and waited for what seemed like the longest hour of my life while the film was being developed. This is where an hour turned into a couple of days full of tears. The security guard who snapped my long-awaited picture actually took a picture of just our bodies - no faces! I was crushed! I cried right there at the counter in the film store and in the car all the way to

D.C. I don't think my poor husband knew what to do, or what to say to help me stop crying. He felt as bad for me as I did.

I got on the car phone and called my dear friend, Rita Belcher, the U.S. secretary for the Smiler Fan Club and told her my sad and disappointing tale. She knew how much it meant to me and of my two other failed attempts and got busy contacting other Smiler members, who she knew were at the show to see if anyone else had caught it on film. Within a week or so, I had not one, but FIVE pictures of Rod and myself up on stage together! Now I really couldn't stop crying, but this time from joy and happiness. I finally had my picture with Mr. Rod Stewart!

Other Smiler member friends of ours from New Jersey later spotted and sent us copies of two local Atlantic City newspapers that described my luck in their reviews of the concert. Richard Weis, in The Press Of Atlantic City, wrote, 'Then there was the banner lady who was a show all by herself. All night long she held up signs and banners with words and phrases ranging from 'Lost in You since '72' to simply 'Celtic.' Near the end of the show's close, she finagled her way onstage to have her picture taken with Stewart, and she even seized the microphone at one point to belt out the chorus of Sam Cooke's 'Twisting The Night Away.' Mr. Stewart, it should be noted, was impressively gracious.' Bob Everland of the casino paper, 'Whoot!' included it in his review also. He noted that it was, 'Undoubtedly a highlight of that woman's evening.' And it certainly was!"

* * *

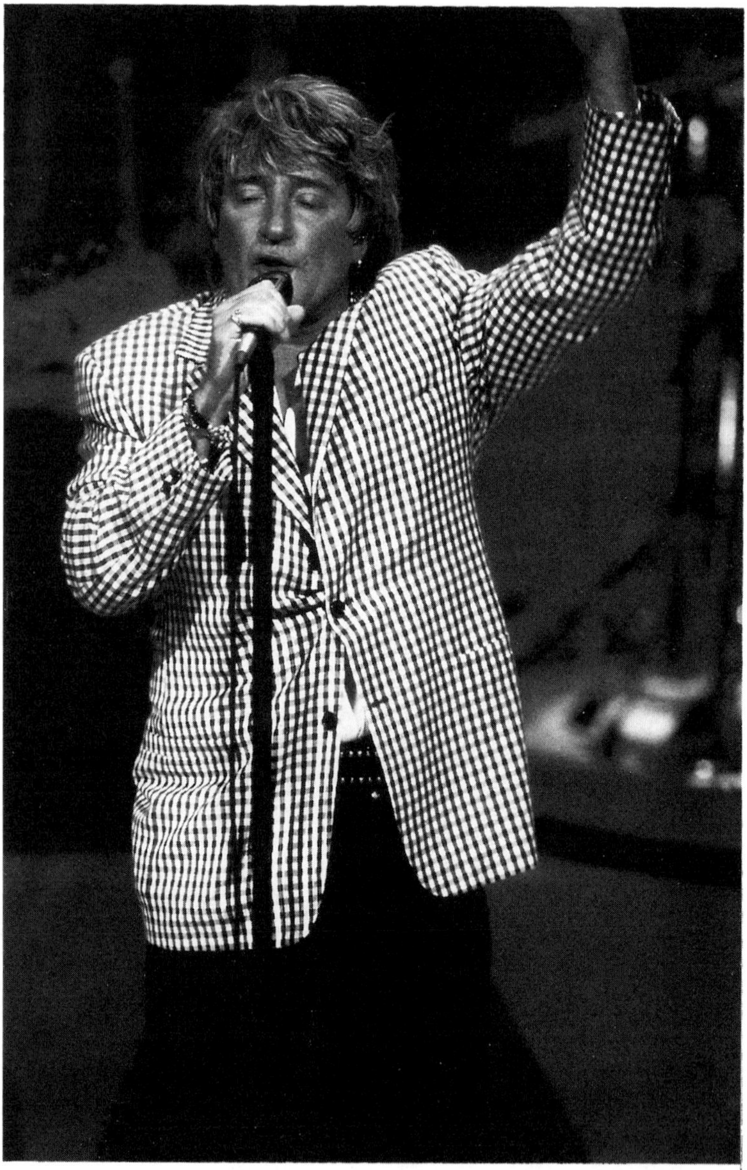

The following three concert reviews and stories are from Rod Stewart fan Ty Turner.

"Well, after almost completely giving up on going to Orlando for the show, my tickets came in. Front row center. I couldn't believe it! I had been having some of the worst luck that anyone could imagine. Needless to say, I was thrilled to find out that my 'birthday wish' came true, and I was off to Orlando (from New Orleans) to see my 'hero.'

My friend that I stayed with in Orlando is not what you would call a 'fan,' but like most of my friends, he has grown to like Rod's music (could it be from being subjected to it every time they are in my car, or at my house?). He was pretty excited to be on the front row of ANY concert! We arrived at the arena very early, as I always like to get there and see the 'fans' come in, just to see the attitudes and the ages that Rod is attracting. I have to say this was my 6th show on the 'New Boys' tour and this was definitely 'my generation.' I didn't notice the diverse ages I saw in New York in September.

Anyway, the usher asked me if she could help me find the seats. She said, 'Oh, this will be easy, FRONT ROW CENTER! What great seats!' We sat down and soon met up with 3 or 4 others from the 'Rodnet!' This is always one of my favorite parts of the show, to get to talk with other real Rod fans.

I work for a clothing company that among other things makes great T-shirts, so I brought one for Mr. Stewart that had a soccer ball on the back made in the same colors as the Scottish flag.

Anyway, as has been reported, the stage 'cover' is

no longer 'When We Were The New Boys,' but is yellow in color and has all the 'hits' printed in red. This kinda told me what we were in store for. Less new stuff, and even more of the same songs we have heard for years. The music started and it was a bit different too. They played 'Maybe It's Because I'm A Londoner' and the Pee Wee Herman song 'Tequila.' Then you hear, I believe it's Ms. Annie Challis' voice say the familiar line 'Ladies and gentlemen, fasten your seatbelts....' and in a flash of the eye, there he stood, right in front of me, the man who's music has been my passion for nearly 27 years, Mr. Stewart himself. He wasn't singing the familiar opener 'Cigarettes and Alcohol,' but the song that has opened many of his shows for the last 22 years 'Hot Legs.' He was wearing black pants and a pink satin shirt. He was thinner than I remember him being on his debut solo tour in 1977! As soon as the curtain had come down, he saw me, and smiled, pointed and sorta rolled his eyes as if to say, 'Oh, jeeze, not HIM again!,' but in a nice sorta way you understand!

Freddie immediately saw me, smiled and said, 'Meet me at the side of the stage after the show!' I said, 'Sure!' He is such a great person. He and I acted silly throughout the show. The show moved on to more of the same hits we have heard throughout the years. 'Some Guys,' 'Forever Young' and an early 'I'm Losing You.'

Then they brought out a white grand piano and Rod did 'The First Cut Is The Deepest,' 'Reason To Believe' and 'You're In My Heart' and one of my all time favorites 'My Heart Can't Tell You No.' As has been said before Rod seemed to not be able to keep his eyes open during these songs. It seemed that if he made eye contact with the audience he would break down. The voice was incredible, truly better than ever, and he leaped and danced around with a big smile on his face, but from my vantage point, I have to say, HE WAS ONLY going through the motions. Yes, Rod's heart is broken, and it shows. That is all I will say about his personal life, but it truly broke my heart to see him so terribly sad!

I had made a banner that said, 'Keep your chin up, old friend, our thoughts are with you' and as I held it up, he walked over and read it, mouthing the words as he read it, and closed his eyes and nodded his head at me.

I later showed him my T-shirt and seeing the soccer ball on the shirt, he said, 'Yes, we love our football!' Later, I thought he was looking right at me and I threw it up to him. His mind must have been elsewhere, because it really startled him, and he immediately threw it back to me, laughing out loud after doing it. I mouthed the words, 'I want you to take it' and he gave me that 'one minute' scolding, which I've learned is his cue to 'I'M NOT TAKING THAT DAMN THING!' So I put it away and just draped my Scottish flag over the railing. When he saw it, he said, 'We love Scotland!'

Towards the end of the show, during 'Having A Party' the big soccer ball hanging from the ceiling opened up and thousands of black and white balloons came showering over us. Having a Party was not the end of the show as usual. He added 'This Old Heart of Mine,' 'The Motown Song,' 'My Girl,' 'Twistin',' and 'Do Ya Think I'm Sexy?' Which the new violinist J'Anna sang the high soprano part on.

At the end of the show, I met Freddie over at the side of the stage, and he took me and my friend backstage. Rod was gone of course, but I had the chance to meet and have a few beers with the band! Freddie took us outside and showed us around their buses.

Rod in Orlando 2/99

Photos by Ty Turner.
Rod at Orlando, Feb. 1999

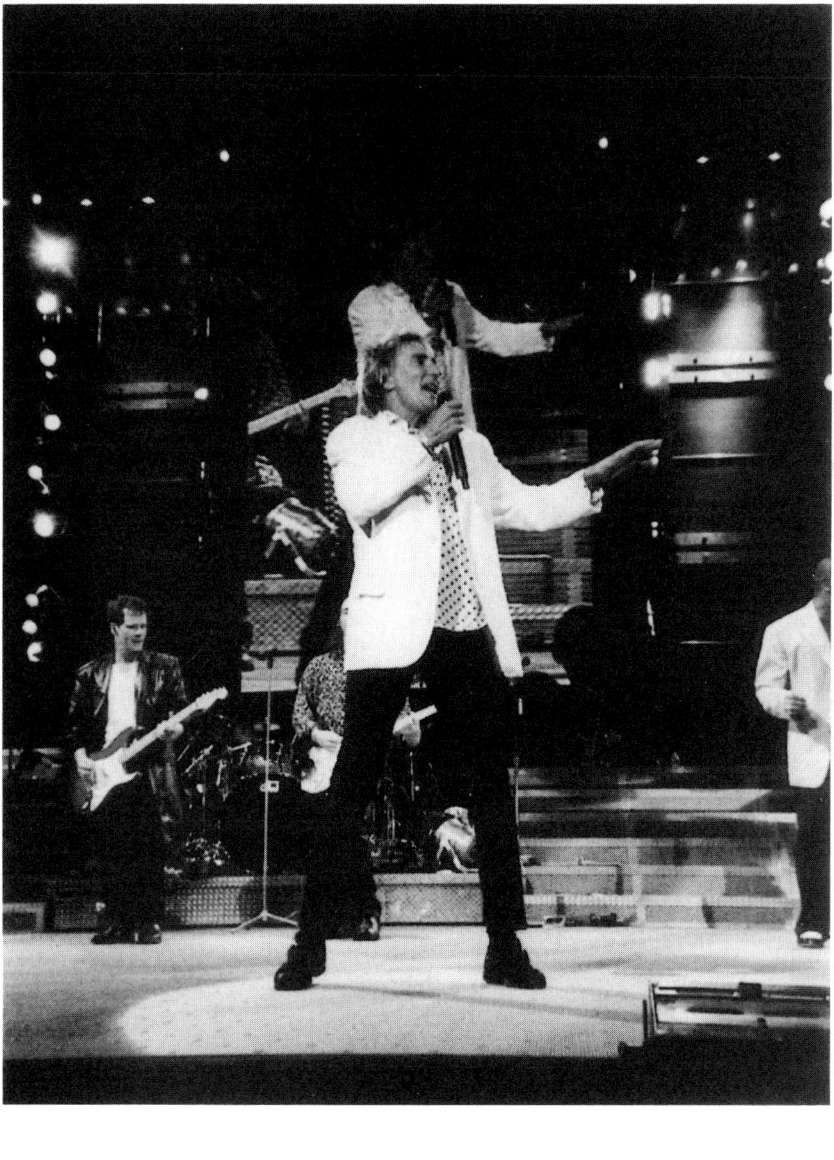

They were moving on that night to the next show, so we said our goodbyes!"

* * *

I got to the concert to pick up my tickets at the will-call desk. I had brought my birth certificate with me because I have 4 names (thanks mom and dad) and they all won't fit on my driver's license and it always poses a problem at the airport. So I thought I'd bring the birth certificate to get the tickets. When I went up to the will-call window, and she said, 'I need to see your license.' I reached for it and realized I had left it back at the house. I said, 'I have my BIRTH CERTIFICATE,' and she said, 'I need a picture.' Long story, but I finally got the tickets.

I ended up with 2nd row center seats. We went in and found lots of Rodfans that I've met online and at show. This is always one of the best parts of the show, it's like a reunion.

Anyway, before you knew it, it was showtime. Annie's voice comes on, 'LADIES AND GENTLEMEN ......HERE'S ROD STEWART!' And the curtain came down and there he was, still the very thin, tanned Rod I saw at the show in Florida, two months ago. But, unlike that show, he was singing, not the ever popular 'Hot Legs,' but 'Tonight I'm Yours.' A song I haven't heard him open with since 1981, but a song that has remained one of my ALL TIME favorite Rod Rockers. Someone had said he used it a week ago, or so as a finale, but I was shocked to hear him open with it! THE CROWD WENT MAD!!

Speaking of the crowd, they were great. This was the first time Rod has played the UNO Lakefront arena since 1988. He had changed to the Superdome, a huge cavernous indoor football stadium, that no one could fill (except Celine Dion...Yuk). The sound is horrible and Rod seems to hate all the empty seats. I was scared that last night would not be a full arena though, because tonight starts Jazz Festival, an event that draws hundreds of thousands of people from around the world for 2 weekends at the end of April and first of May each year. However, as I looked around, I could see it was close to a sell out. Security was almost nonexistent, and before you know it, people on row two joined people in row one against the railing at the front of the stage. No one seemed to mind. Row 3 was empty, so I had brought 8 people from work with me and they were back on row 14. I went back and told them they should come to the front, some did, some said they would stay back. One of the girls (this was her first Rod show) who stayed in row 14 caught a soccer ball. She said, 'Ty, it was like it was in slow motion, I saw it coming to me, and I fell back in my seat and it landed in my lap.' Some gals have all the luck!

Rod was in great voice. He seemed to, again in my opinion, put on a happy face and move and jump and dance and twirl the microphone stand like the great entertainer that he is. But behind it, it still seems like he is not really there. He doesn't seem to truly be having a great time. I don't know if it is just because we KNOW what he is going through right now, or the fact that I saw him twice last year at Madison Square Garden, and nothing could ever compare to those shows, or perhaps as with most things it is a combination of both. People brought him Mardi Gras beads and he would take them and walk around with them in his hands. One girl brought him a Rod-doll that looked uncannily like the real thing. There were the flowers, stuffed animals and flags as usual. One girl that I met online and at the shows brought him some beautiful roses with a Celtic scarf (I believe) wrapped around them, he took them and she FINALLY got HER soccer ball! I was thrilled. There were 3 girls that were brought up to sing background for 'Rocks,' something I haven't seen him do since the New York shows. They had their 3 minutes of fame, literally! He pulled a few girls up from the audience during 'Having A Party,' but he wasn't done yet. He did 'Maggie Mae,' and 'Twistin'' after they returned to their seats, which was a little different.

I had made him some Mardi Gras beads in 'Celtic Green' and actually found tiny soccer balls to string on them. He FINALLY saw them and took them and put them on. He seemed to like them. I also had made a banner that was a take off on the one I showed him in Orlando, 'Keep Your Chin Up Old Friend, Our Thoughts Are With You.' For this one I scanned the cartoon of him pulling his pants down at a restaurant in England and I added the caption, 'Keep your CHIN up and your TROUSERS down!' He came to the edge of the stage, read it and laughed and grabbed his big silver buckle, acting like he was going to de-pants himself right there. Very funny!

Anyway, as usual, all good things come to an end, and it was over. It was an all in all great show! All I can say is I hope Rod finds true happiness again in his life, for all the happiness he brings to me and millions of others, he truly deserves it."

* * *

"I was shocked to read on AOL News that Rod planned on performing at the Houston International Rodeo Show! Rod Stewart at a RODEO SHOW, I asked! I immediately went to the web site for the Houston International Rodeo Show to find out it was graced with performances by legends like Tony Bennett! So I went about planning to get tickets! I emailed Cyber Club and was told no tickets would be available for this show! I'll spare you the long ordeal, but when tickets went on sale for the general public, the only thing available was in section 700 of the Astrodome. The Astrodome is the oldest indoor football arena built in the United States, and is 33 years old. It seats about 65,000 and is in a word CAVERNOUS! The 700 section seats are so far away from the center of the field that you might as well be in another town. Of course I've gotten kind of used to front row seats for Mr. Stewart, so I went about trying to get 'scalper seats!' This rodeo show was for charity and the seats were being sold for $10-$12.00 a piece. I ended up paying $230 for 3 tickets from a scalper! They were 3rd row off the floor! Still a ways from center stage! At the last minute Cyber Club offered rodfans a chance to win about 20 tickets for standing floor tickets, but I was unable to win any!

So I packed my cowboy boots and headed off to Houston with a friend of mine that likes Mr. Stewart, but is not a fan. I live about 250 miles from there, in Louisiana, and I met up with another friend between New Orleans and Houston and we got into Houston about 3:00 in the afternoon. It's kind of surreal when you drive into a huge city like Houston (about 4th largest in the U.S.) and think, 'Well, here we go again, another big city and Rod's here somewhere!'

We got to our hotel, changed and headed off to meet up with about 20 fellow Rod fans that had traveled from as far away as the New York area to see Mr. Stewart perform! We had a few beers and it was off to the show! The time for the Rodeo Show to start was 7:00 pm, and we had been told that Mr. Stewart would hit the stage about 9:10, so after finding our seats I went about trying to run into Freddie White, one of Mr. Stewart's background singers who has become a friend that never fails to come over and chat with me before, and during the show.

I was unable to run into him or anyone else in the show, so I went out and rode carnival rides with a friend, which had been set up around the dome. You see, I was totally uninterested in the bull riding, calf roping show that was going on down on the dirt floor that was once a football field! About 8:30 pm I made my way back into the arena and purchased a couple of Rod T-shirts that were printed up for the Vegas show and I made my way to my seat!

At this point the rodeo show was about to end. The announcer said, 'I'd like to make an announcement, ROD STEWART IS IN THE HOUSE! The crowd went wild. I would estimate the crowd at that point to be about 35,000, the arena was about half full. My friend that went with me said she thought a lot of these 'cowboys' would be leaving when Mr. Stewart came on. Boy! Was she wrong!

By the time I got there the entire band was on the stage. The stage was not Mr. Stewart's regular stage, but a round stage that is used for the entire week long rodeo show. It has two columns on one side of the circle and it rotates so that everyone gets a decent view. It sat way on the other side of the floor, but, as I thought would happen, it began to be pushed to the center of the dirt field, with all the band on board! I was shocked to see the entire band had come for the show. I never imagined that Mr. Stewart would bring the whole group, or that they would all be available to come, but low and behold, here they were! I had brought my Scottish flag and I began to hold it up and wave at Freddie, and even though he was wearing his glasses, he couldn't see me, we were still so far away!

At this point I glanced around the arena, and much to my surprise it had filled to nearly capacity (I estimated correctly, I might add to be about 57,000, the largest crowd I have ever been in the middle of to see Mr. Stewart! And come to think of it, why wouldn't it be filled to the top! Mr. Stewart comes to Houston at least twice per tour, but tickets go for nearly $100 plus, here the Houston residents had the chance to see the greatest Rock & Roller of all time for about $12, and before the night was over, they would indeed get their money's worth plus more!

After the stage had made it's way to the center of the field, the lights went down, and out of the side of the arena came a big white Suburban Truck! It pulled right up to the edge of the stage, and out walked Mr. Stewart! Quite different from the limousine that we usually see him get out of! He made his way to the stage (through the dirt and cow dung) and in a blink of an eye was standing center stage singing 'Tonight I'm Yours!' Big screens were above the stage and you could see on his face he was very nervous, and looked and probably felt a bit out of his element. By the time he got to 'Some Guys Have All The Luck,' you could tell he was warming up to the idea of playing the rodeo and the crowd were warming up to him!

He looked great, much like the pictures I saw from his show in Las Vegas back on January 1st! Hair a bit longer and darker with definite highlights of light blonde. Very spiky, with what a hair professional called 'trenches' cut into it! He was definitely 'thicker, heavier' than he was the weeks after he broke up with Rachel and was on the road last year! He had on a white shirt, an off white vest and the trademark black tuxedo pants that he wore during the entire tour the last two years! His shoes were red velvet with buckles on the side, no cow dung on them I noticed! He made one costume change into a black silky shirt.

The crowd were very much into the music and Mr.

Stewart. Some were upset that the entire stadium didn't stand up, but you have to realize this was not the typical Rod Stewart crowd and all 57,000 were in seats that were what seemed to be a mile from the stage. All the cowboys and cowgirls around me were tapping their feet and singing along. There were pockets of diehard fans that were standing and dancing throughout the arena and that was fun to look around and watch for. During the song 'Some Guys Have All The Luck' about 1000 folks were allowed to come out from under the seats to stand in front of the barricaded stage.

After 'Maggie Mae' Mr. Stewart walked down from the stage, hopped into the big Suburban truck and left the field! I knew at this point there was to be no encore! It all lasted about an hour and a half and then it was over. It was a very good and different kind of concert!

***

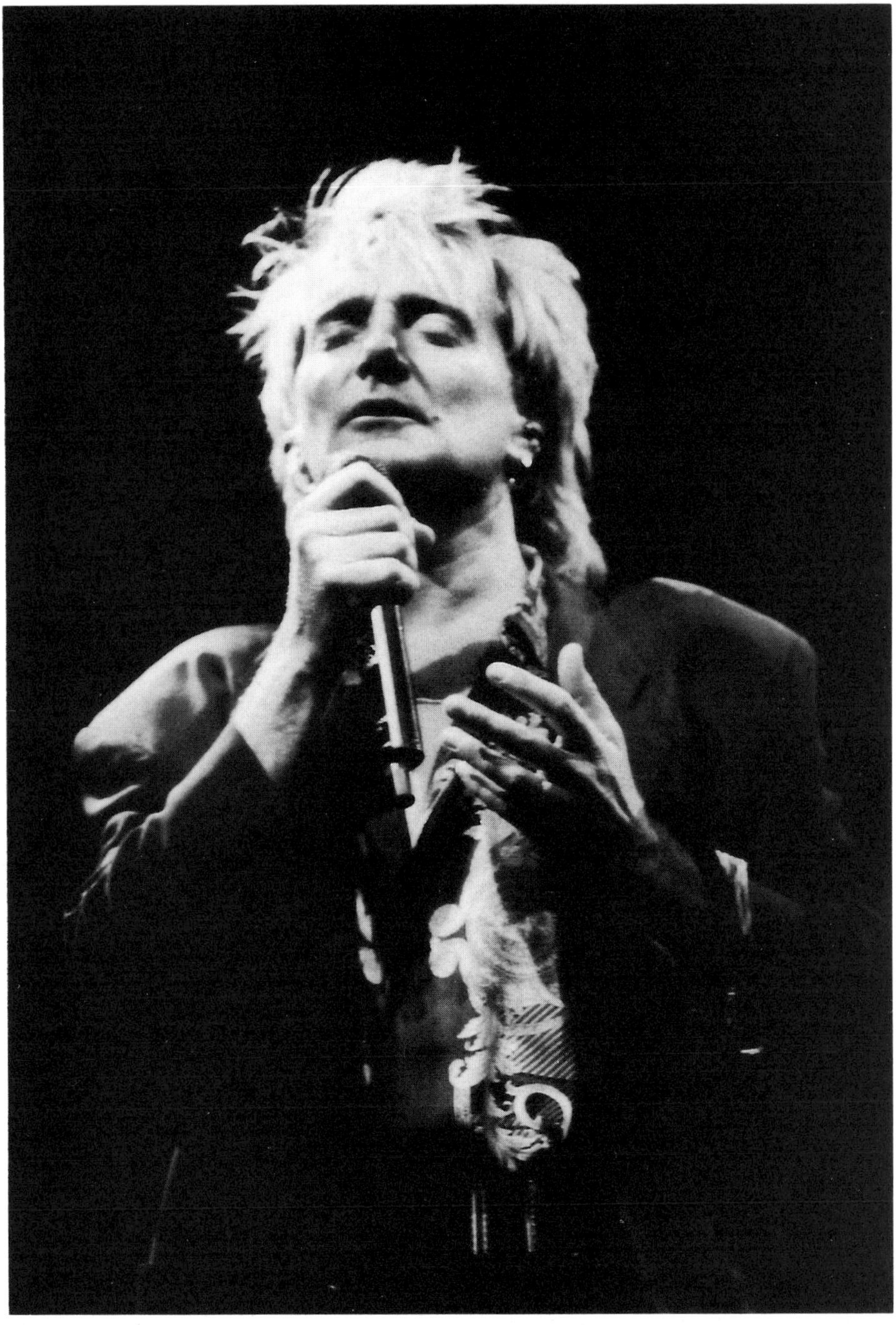

'Out of Order' Tour.

'Out of Order' Tour.

'Out of Order' Tour.

'Out of Order' Tour.

Rod Stewart Survey

Thanks to Tracy and her Rod website which is at; http://members.aol.com/maggie1971/rasar.html for allowing me permission to reprint her survey. For those of you who like surveys this is one that is well done and quite informative.

This survey ran from Oct. 1997 to June 1999. There were 801 participants. All answers were optional so not all results are from all 801 people.

Sex

male.............228
female..........564

Age

under 18..............71
18-30...................209
31-40...................296
over 40...............217

How long you've been a fan

before the 70's...............86
since 70's......................423
since 80's......................156
since 90's......................113

Favorite Song

(All songs with more than three votes are listed)

Maggie May..................................117
You're In My Heart......................67
Forever Young.............................55
I Was Only Joking.......................51
Tonight's The Night....................38
Do Ya Think I'm Sexy.................23
Have I Told You Lately...............22
First Cut Is The Deepest.............20
Hot Legs.......................................20
Reason To Believe......................20
Mandolin Wind...........................19
Broken Arrow..............................15
Downtown Train........................12
Stay With Me...............................12
Passion...11
Every Picture Tells A Story.........10
Ooh La La....................................10
Sailing..10
You Wear It Well..........................9
For The First Time........................8
I Don't Want To Talk About It......8
Lost In You....................................8
My Heart Can't Tell You...............8
Some Guys Have All The Luck...8
Killing of Georgie.........................7
This Old Heart Of Mine...............7
Young Turks..................................6
Handbags And Gladbags............5
I'm Losing You..............................5
Motown Song................................5
Muddy Sam And Otis..................5
Baby Jane......................................4
If Loving You Is Wrong................4
People Get Ready.........................4

Least Favorite Song

(Again, all songs with more than three votes are listed)

Do Ya Think I'm Sexy..................55
Infatuation...................................22
Have I Told You Lately.................18
Killing Of Georgie.........................17
Maggie May..................................16
Hot Legs.......................................15
Sailing..15
Love Touch...................................13
Passion..13
Downtown Train............................9
Ghetto Blaster................................9
Pinball Wizard...............................9
Tom Trauberts Blues......................9
Camouflage...................................7
People Get Ready.........................7
Broken Arrow................................6
Cigarettes And Alcohol.................6
Leave Virginia Alone.....................6
Baby Jane......................................4
Forever Young...............................4
Rocks...4
Tonight's The Night.......................4

Favorite Album
(I listed all this time)

Unplugged And Seated............................65
Out Of Order...51
If We Fall In Love Tonight......................40
Spanner In The Works............................40
Footloose And Fancy Free.....................34
Vagabond Heart......................................33
Every Picture Tells A Story.....................32
When We Were The New Boys.............29
Storyteller...26
Blondes Have More Fun........................25
Greatest Hits...21
Atlantic Crossing....................................18
A Night On The Town...........................12
Downtown Train (selections).................11
Absolutely Live..9
Foolish Behavior......................................9
Smiler...8
Gasoline Alley..6
A Nod Is As Good As A Wink (Faces)....5
Body Wishes..5
Mercury Anthology.................................5
Never A Dull Moment............................5
Tonight I'm Yours....................................5
Ooh La La (Faces)...................................3
Sing It Again..3
Rod Stewart, Every Beat Of My Heart....2
Long Player (Faces).................................1
Snakes And Ladders (Faces)...................1
Truth (Faces)..1

135

Have you seen a show?

yes......................................608
no...26
no, but want to................136

How many shows have you seen?

1 - 3 Shows................................298
4 - 6 Shows................................123
7 - 10 Shows..............................99
11-15 Shows...............................45
16 plus.......................................56

Favorite shows
(Listed by year/tour)

1970-75 (Rod & Faces)..................17
1976/77..3
1978/79 (Blondes Tour)................10
1980/81 (World Tour)...................13
1983 (Body Wishes)........................8
1984 (Camouflage)..........................8
1985/86..13
1987..2
1988/89 (Out of Order)................55
1991/92 (Vagabond Heart).........39
1993/94 (Unplugged)...................53
1995/96 (Spanner)......................125
1997 (Songs & Visions)..................3
1998 (All Rod Tour).....................82
1999 (All Hits)...............................45

Where do you live?
(Rod fans span the globe)

Argentina..6
Austria..3
Australia...9
Barcelona..1
Belgium..1
Brazil..2
Canada..57
Denmark..4
Dominican Republic................................1
England..41
Finland...2
Germany..3
Holland..4
Hungary...1
India...2
Indonesia...3
Ireland...4
Italy..1
Lithuania...1
Malaysia..1
Malta...1
Mexico..4
New Zealand..9
Netherlands..1
Norway...4
Poland...2

(continued)

Scotland..9
Singapore...3
South Africa...1
Spain...1
Sweden...9
Switzerland..2
Thailand...2
Turkey...1
United States....................................555
Uruguay...1
Venezuela...1

In the US, the States who responded the most were ....

California...55
Ohio..45
New York...43
New Jersey..38
Pennsylvania......................................38
Virginia..26
Texas...25
Florida..25
North Carolina...................................19
Tennessee..18
Kentucky..17
Maryland...17
Michigan..17
Illinois..13
Connecticut...10
Indiana...10
Georgia...10

Louisiana..9
Missouri..9
Oklahoma...9
South Carolina...9
Washington..9
Massachusetts..8
Mississippi..8
Wisconsin..8
Colorado..7
Alabama..6
West Virginia..6
Arkansas..5
Iowa...5
New Hampshire......................................5
Maine...4
Minnesota...4
Utah...4

Some comments that were received:

* "I'm ready to bring in the year 2000 with ROD in Las Vegas!!"

* "It's always a good night for me after a Rod show!"

* "Rod's in MY heart!"

* "Least favorite song...Nothing of Rod's!"

* "A Nod Is As Good As A Wink, from Rod! He nodded at me during a show in 1996!"

* "Favorite song......Is this a trick question?"

Autograph party.

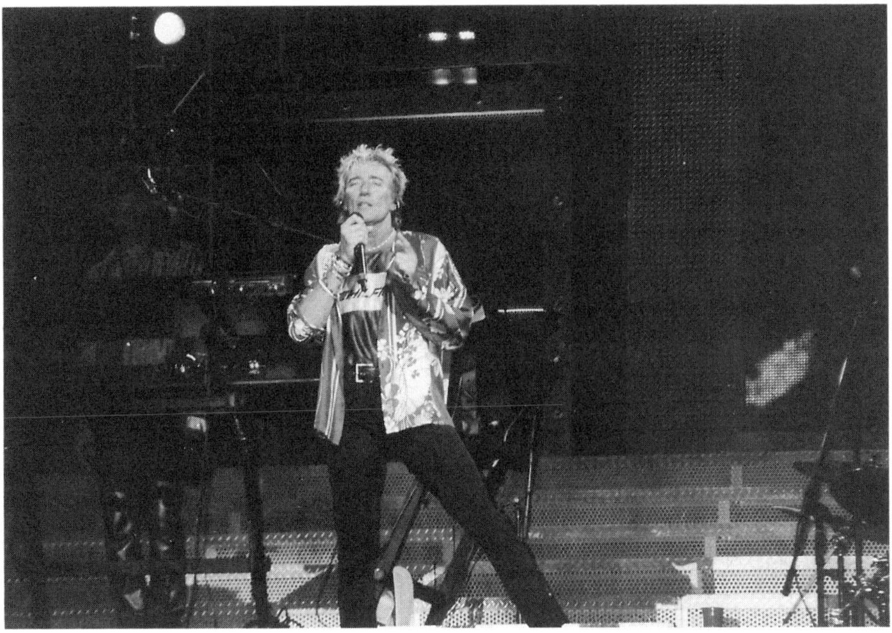

Penthouse Interview With Rod Stewart

It's sometimes interesting to read an interview someone did a number of years ago to see what was said, what came to pass and if the person has changed their views. Here are excerpts from a 1975 interview Rod did with Penthouse Magazine. It was reprinted in Issue #36 of Smiler Magazine if the reader would like to see the interview in its' entirety.

Penthouse: What else are you crazy about besides football and being partly Scottish - that's all we seem to read about in the papers.

Stewart: That's 'cos it's all everybody asks me about. I wouldn't say they were the two main things in my life. I'm interested in lots of things.

Penthouse: What sort of girls do you like?

Stewart: They have to be tall - can't stand short girls. I like them the same height as me - 5 ft. 11 ins. - with shoes on. After that I go for intelligence. Then I start looking at everything else. Those two primarily. I mean we all want everything. You can go on looking for years can't you?

Penthouse: Why do you like intelligent women?

Stewart: I need to be expanded by a woman.

Penthouse: Do the girl fans throw themselves at you?

Stewart: Bits of girls, yeah.

Penthouse: It must give you a weird impression of women when they chase you rather than you chase them.

Stewart: I don't know why they do it meself. Can't understand it meself [laughs]. I don't like to be chased around the country-side though.

Penthouse: Do you have girls who follow you everywhere, wherever you go - sort of super fans?

Stewart: Super-fans! Oh yeah! Always get plenty of those - male and female. There's a couple every gig - you get to recognize them.

Penthouse: How does your steady girl Dee Harrington take all this?

Stewart: She don't, 'cos she don't know.... Well, she does know. I tell you it's going to get a lot worse before it gets better.

Penthouse: Is she still living with you in Ascot?

Stewart: Not at this moment in time, though she

might be next week.

Penthouse: You have a lot of bust-ups with Dee. How do you come together again?

Stewart: We just drift into the same place at the same time.

Penthouse: If you're always splitting up, the relationship must worry you.

Stewart: Nothing worries me actually, nothing at all worries me.

Penthouse: Are you happy having Dee around, or do you feel she cramps your style?

Stewart: No. She's a good sport. I trust her immensely. She must have something about her that we come together.

Penthouse: She certainly have fantastic resilience.

Stewart: She's got a lot of things fantastic about her 'cos I keep going back to her. But the trouble is we want our cake and we want to be able to eat it as well. I'm footloose at the moment, but I expect we'll get back together.

Penthouse: Does she want to marry you?

Stewart: I don't think so, but girls always say that don't they, when they're on the spot? They always say I don't want to marry you anyway. But I wouldn't be a bad catch you know!

Penthouse: But you obviously intend to eventually marry.

Stewart: Why do you say obviously?

Penthouse: Because I think that basically you've got a very traditional outlook on life.

Stewart: Yeah, I'm always the guv'nor. But I need to have a woman by my side - always. I like women. I'm very fond of women I must say.

Penthouse: Do you think you'd find it difficult to be faithful if you did get married?

Stewart: No, not at all. That's why I'm not married now, because I know I couldn't be faithful.

Penthouse: So you'll know that special girl when you meet her?

Stewart: Oh yeah! A bell will ring, the clouds will open up and the sun will come bursting through - in the middle of winter at six o'clock in the evening!

Penthouse: What's the reason for your popularity in the States?

Stewart: I dunno, it's difficult to analyze, but I'd like to think it's because I make good records! We've just done a million on the last album in the States. It didn't do as well as the last two, but then I sold more albums in the rest of Europe. But so much of the reason for our popularity in the States is to do with the visual appearance of the band. That's half the battle I'm sure. But it's not really for me to say is it?

Penthouse: What do sales in America mean to you?

Stewart: Well it makes a lot of money for me. It bought my Ascot house. It's very difficult to become very wealthy just working in England or Europe.

Penthouse: Joe Cocker, another popular British singer in the States, has reportedly ruined his voice. Is this your fear?

Stewart: Well, it shouldn't get that far! But a lot of trouble that people get with their voices is usually psychological anyway. If you think your voice is going to go it will. I daresay half way through the American tour I shall get the panics. Me voice is going to go! Ooh! Ooh! Ooh!

Penthouse: So what will you do about it?

Stewart: Drink a little bit more! But if it does go I'll just run round the stage a bit more. Put all the energys in another was see, and give them a bit more show than usual.

Penthouse: But it is a fact that you can get nodules on the vocal chords through over-doing it.

Stewart: Yeah. That happened to Gary Glitter. He had 'em. He thought he had cancer. They were working him like hell. In the old days he used to do five or six hours a night. Nobody makes me work hard. I do an hour and a half a night, five nights a week. Then that's it! Forget it!

Penthouse: Are you ever compared with Mick Jagger?

Stewart: They did three years ago. You had to put your hand on your hip to be compared with Mick Jagger then. It's different now. Nobody compares me with him now.

Penthouse: Do you admire him as an artist?

Stewart: As a writer more than anything else - as a lyricist.

Penthouse: Now that the dust has settled a little on 'Smiler,' what do you think of it?

Stewart: It doesn't stand up to 'Gasoline Alley' which didn't sell the most, but that's not the hallmark of a good album is it? You can't please yourself, everyone else, and also sell a lot. The last three sold more than 'Gasoline Alley.' If I was to release 'Gasoline' next week it would do well because I wasn't known outside a smallish circle in those days.

Penthouse: What do you say to critics who say you got too much too easily?

Stewart: I don't think anybody would deny me my money.

Penthouse: Does it sometimes take a while to realize how much you are worth? That you can literally

have anything you want?

Stewart: I've always been the same even when I had no money. I'd move heaven and hell to get what I wanted. I suppose it's still in me now. But it depresses me. I think why should you want a car that does 200 miles an hour. I suppose there's a slight feeling of guilt that I'm not worth that money, in spite of the fact I've earned it all myself - with some help of course. You suddenly think to yourself, am I really worth all that money? One day in the week I get depressed and think ####ing hell why do people come to see me? You don't quite realize you're....talented, you know? Then sometimes you realize how good you are. Being a Capricorn as well you need to be told how good you are. If somebody tells me I'm good I really get a buzz out of it.

Penthouse: Harry Secombe once said that he's always expecting a 'hone call and there'll be a man on the line saying that it's all over and that he's got to 'send it all back.' Do you ever get this feeling?

Stewart: I suppose Secombe has had the same amount of success as I have. It's been a gradual progression. It hasn't been sudden overnight stardom. It didn't happen when I was a silly age either. It happened in 1970 when I was 26, right?

Penthouse: Other pop stars have got involved with mystical religions. Meher Baba for instance..

Stewart: ###k all that! That silly old sod! That's what led my mate Ronnie Lane adrift. Meher Baba! Ha! I didn't go in for all that flower-power-if-you're-going to San Francisco thing. Load of codswallop and rubbish! I've got me own sort of religion really. I'm quite a puritan at heart I suppose.

Penthouse: What do you mean, puritan?

Stewart: Well, I think there is some 'thing' somewhere. I don't think it's in the shape of ourselves either. I dunno. I've got a set of rules which is my religion I suppose.

Penthouse: What are those rules?

Stewart: Well, it's private. I'd be embarrassed.

Penthouse: Well try to overcome your embarrassment.

Stewart: It's appreciation of one's mother and father......and things like that.

Penthouse: As a Capricorn go-getter, are you basically a materialist?

Stewart: I suppose I am, yeah.

Penthouse: Are you afraid of death?

Stewart: I was at one stage of my life. That's why I started as a grave digger, you probably know that. I was scared of dying so I thought the only way round this is to go and work in a cemetery. It kicked it out of me.

Penthouse: How did it do that? You weren't seeing

death, only the result. You weren't seeing suffering.

Stewart: No, true, but there's the suffering of the people standing round watching the coffin going in the ground and crying and all the business going on. Going and watching someone suffer in a hospital isn't going to knock it out of you. I'm not scared of dying."

* * *

Rod and Rachel.

On the following 15 pages I have reproduced a special Birthday Present that was given to Rod Stewart on January 10, 1997 by a group of his fans.

It was in booklet form and expressed Birthday Wishes and what Rod's music has meant to them. I think it could also represent what many others feel as well.

Rod Stewart - Making Smilers Smile

Happy Birthday

1-10-97

Rod Stewart - Making Smilers Smile

Table of Contents

Forward..Ty Turner
⚽..Ty Turner
⚽⚽...Jan James
⚽⚽⚽..Tracey Rasar
⚽⚽⚽⚽..Janice Bernhard
⚽⚽⚽⚽⚽..Debbie Heile
⚽⚽⚽⚽⚽⚽...Nancy & Bob Garcia
⚽⚽⚽⚽⚽⚽⚽...Susan Green
⚽⚽⚽⚽⚽⚽⚽⚽..MarieKo
⚽⚽⚽⚽⚽⚽⚽⚽⚽..Rita Belcher
⚽⚽⚽⚽⚽⚽⚽⚽⚽⚽..Steve and Kimberly
⚽⚽⚽⚽⚽⚽⚽⚽⚽⚽⚽...Peggy Ripley

January 10, 1997

154

Forward

First off, I have to say, I am going to have a hard time writing this forward and calling you *Rod*! With the great deal of respect I have for you, and being a southern gentleman, my soul wants to refer to you as *Mr. Stewart*! However, in a recent interview you said that you have a hard time calling us *fans*, that you prefer the term *friends*, and since this group of Smilers looks on you as a friend, I hope you don't mind that I refer to you as *ROD*!

When I was asked to compile this gift to you I was proud that the group entrusted this project to me, but I wasn't sure I wanted to do it.

But as the letters to you started coming in, I realized how interesting this was going to be. You see Rod, we are a very close knit group of *Smilers!* Though we all come from different walks of life, and different areas of the country, we all have one tie that binds us closely together, YOU, and I believe THAT is the message that we would like to convey to you through the pages of this brochure. Rod, you have a way of bringing people together, that we feel, no other entertainer can do.

Most of us have been fans for over 20 years. We have watched you perform, and we have watched you grow, and mature. Of course, at the same time, we were growing, and maturing, and watching your every move. Therefore it was inevitable that you would have a big influence on the development of our personality.

Back in the 70's you burst on the scene as a poet in song, in the same class as Bob Dylan. You were recognized as a gregarious, charismatic person that had a way with words that touched the heart's of your listeners. Then in the late 70's critics focused on your *Hollywood lifestyle* and seemed to miss the message of your music, though, as you have admitted, this was in some ways your own fault. However, in the 80's that message proved to be strong, as we saw with the release of *Tonight I'm Yours*! Once again, the critics raved about your work, and we were **proud**!

In the 90's you met your soul mate, and became a wonderful example of a superstar that was still in touch with the important things in life, family, friends and unselfish concern for your fellowman. We know that though much of your charitable works go unreported, you are very active in helping others.

So, Rod, what we'd like to say to you on your 52nd birthday is, Thanks for being such a fun, caring soulful person. Thanks for being such a wonderful entertainer, and bringing smiles to our faces everyday as we listen to your music, watch your videos and attend your concerts. Thanks for being someone that we can be proud to say that we are fans of, and......**THANK YOU ROD FOR THE *SOUNDS YOU MAKE!***

Ty Turner

Jan James

Dear Rod

Well I wanted you to know that I was thinking of you on your birthday, but you already know that if you get the feedback from the Warner Bros. web site called Rod Stewart's Lounge. I sent you a Happy Birthday there too.

I hope you had a super day and got to enjoy your family.

By the way...do you still have that crazy blue banner from Lafayette, LA? The one that says if god was a rock singer, his name would be ROD! Well I made that thing and took it to New York last March where all the Smilers at the party at Kennedy's signed. Well at the risk of boring you out of your mind, I wanted to tell you the rest of that story. I, a charming, sweet lady, really, your own age, got kicked out of the show in Lafayette by security because I didn't return to my seat when told to do so. Well, as I was being escorted out, I gave the banner to my friend, Pam, who after working very hard managed to give it to you. You graciously gave her an autographed ball in exchange for the banner, and, being a true friend, she gave the ball to me.. Of course, that means she doesn't have a ball. I really wish there was some way she could get a ball too. She's also a Smiler and has been a fan for many years.

Pam and I also saw you in New Orleans on this tour and thoroughly enjoyed the show. Rod, you amaze me with your energy level. I am also a kid at heart, like you, but don't think I could follow you around the stage for half the show, much less the whole. Anyway, I know you have lots of well-wishers wishes to read, so I'll sign off...again...HAPPY BIRTHDAY!!!

Keep making music, Love you,

Jan James

Tracey Rasar

Dear Rod

Hello!! Let me take this time to THANK YOU for all the memories you have given me over the last 20 years. I have been a fan since I was 12 years old and bought my first album with my baby sitting money. That album was Foot Loose and Fancy Free. Since then I look forward to each new release with great anticipation.

My first concert wasn't until 1989 and it was terrific! Since then I have seen you 7 times.....like a fine wine you get better with age!! This past year I took my 6 year old daughter, who is also a big fan of yours with me to see you in Detroit. This was as big of thrill for me as it was for her. I had a tear in my eye as she stood on her chair and danced and sang the whole show.

Thank you for taking time out to read all of our thoughts and memories you are a great man!

Take Care and Keep on Rockin'......Love ya',

> **Tracey**

PS I gave you the black and gold soccer boxers in Virginia Beach last May, I hope you and Rachel enjoyed them!!

Janice Bernhard

Dear Rod,

It is my honor to wish you a very happy birthday and a healthy, enjoyable new year. As I look back on the countless instances where your music has brought so much joy to my life, I can only hope these few words can adequately express my gratitude and respect for your talent. The love and respect for your music has touched every area of my life and has brought together, through the internet, people whose lives may never otherwise have crossed. Meaningful friendships have developed which have made the experience of your music even stronger.

I had the privilege of seeing six concerts during your last tour. Although each show was phenomenal, several memories from the Cleveland concert stand out. That concert was a few days after the Madison Square Garden concerts were canceled. I had traveled to New York for the concerts so I took a computer mad banner to Cleveland saying "Hey Rod! Smiler Missed You in NYC!". During *Maggie May* you came over and read the banner, bowed to me, smiled, and pointed to your throat. It was so kind of you to acknowledge me like that! My mother also came to that concert with me (her first Rod Stewart concert). We were both standing at the rail during *Soothe Me* and were lucky enough to have you touch our hands. My mother was elated! I could just see it in here eyes! I will never forget that moment. Although I have never had the opportunity to meet you, I was able to meet the band in Pittsburg and again at Le Bar Bat in New York City. It was a dream come true for me. I'm sure I don't have to tell you that you have a wonderful and talented group of people working with you. Lastly, it has been such a pleasure traveling to different cities and meeting people that have the same appreciation for you and your music that I do. There is a spirit of camaraderie among us that is not easily found elsewhere and I'm proud to have these new friends in my life.

In closing, I want to thank you for taking the time to read this note and wish you and your family all the happiness you deserve.

Thank You Rod for the Sounds You Make!

Janice

Debbie Heile

Dear Rod,

    What can I write that you haven't heard a "thousand" times before, except to say that even though I have heard your songs a "thousand" times before, they still result in a special thrill for me. Over the years, you have always been there for my enjoyment and excitement, never failing me. Your concerts are invigorating and inspiring, leaving me passionate and fervent, emotions that my husband, Rick, would like to thank you for!!
    I love that you take the time to acknowledge your fans, and make us feel special. You are an extraordinary man for doing so, and I especially love those few minutes you gave to me last November in Boston at the C.D. signing. I hope you comprehend how much opportunities like these mean to those of us who have followed you for years.
    Please continue to "carry on" for many more years and keep us all RODHOT with anticipation and delight. For indeed, you are in my soul!

With forever love,

Debbie Heilie

Nancy Garcia

Dear Mr. Rod Stewart,

I would like to wish you a very Happy 52nd. Birthday from one Capricorn to another! I hope your special day was good to you!

As I sit here trying to continue, I find the words very hard to put on paper. I had the same experience when my husband Bob and I went to your New York Signing. When it was my turn to have my CD signed you asked me who should you make it out too? I said Nancy, thank you and thank you for all the years of great music. That is what I came up with, after waiting outside for 5 hours. After we had our turns getting our CD's signed - I thought to myself, after 5 hours, that is all you can say to a man that you respect and love with all your heart!!!

So now I would like to express to you what I wanted to say, but couldn't. You have filled our hearts and our home with your many years of great music. Being part of your fan club allows us to feel a little bit closer to you. All the Smiler members are family, no matter where they live and we all love hearing about every inch of your life, past, present and we are all waiting to hear about your next tour in the near future 1998. If there are articles written in magazines, an interview coming up or a TV show that you are going to appear on, etc., we all run to purchase, or set our VCR's. That is because we all feel that we can not have or get enough of ROD!!!

I will end my letter to you wishing you the very best in all areas of your life and I wish the same for your family -you have always given so much of yourself to all of our lives.

Again.... Happy Birthday Rod

Love ya,

Nancy and Bob Garcia

Susan Green

Happy Birthday Rod!!!

Your life has touched mine and many others in ways that you will never know!
You have made a mark in time that will continue on forever!

Thank you for making this world a sweeter place to live.

May sunshine and happiness surround you always!

Love,

Susan Green

Marie Ko

HAPPY BIRTHDAY, ROD

A very happy birthday. Thank you for all the music you have given us. Your music has been a very important part of my life, from the ballads to the hot rocking songs. There is not one day that I am not listening or singing one of your songs. Thank you for your gift of music.

My first concert was at the Camouflage tour, and I haven't missed one yet. Your concerts are one place where everyone is friendly with each other, has a terrific time singing and rocking away with you. Everyone is there for one purpose, to enjoy the voice, movements and music of the great Rod Stewart, who gives his all to his fans.

You probably don't remember that at your recent tour in San Jose, California there was this little old short Asian jumping up and down holding a banner and dancing away to your music. That was me, 59 years old; that night I was a teenager again for one evening with you. I jumped, screamed and danced the entire evening. Rod, you make your fans feel Forever Young and we love you for it.

I'd like to let you know that we have three generations of Rod fans here; my daughter, her girls, and me. I have often seen many three-generations of Rod fans at your concerts - proves how terrific you are.

Because of you, Smiler fans from many areas of the United States have gotten together on chat and by e-mail on the internet, and have also met in New York for the first time. We have formed a great friendship because of you. Our group's wildest fantasy is to be able to meet you in New York in May of 97. I think if this would become a reality I would have died and gone to Rod heaven.

Again, thank you, thank you Rod, for the many years of music. HAPPY BIRTHDAY, ROD!!! My sincere best wishes to you, your beautiful family and beautiful wife, Rachel.

Marie Ko

Rita Belcher

JANUARY 10, 1997 HAPPY BIRTHDAY ROD !
WE LOVE YOU !!

"TONIGHT'S THE NIGHT" we honor your birthday. I decided to do this tribute to you using the titles to some of my favorite songs you have given us through the years. I must say for 52, "YOU WEAR IT WELL" and we all know that you will always be "FOREVER YOUNG".

Rod, this last tour was a dream tour for me. I attended your shows in Charlotte, both shows in Philly, Pittsburg, the first New York City shows (sorry you were sick), Raleigh, NC, Virginia Beach and the final show of the tour in Boston and I "HAD ME A REAL GOOD TIME". I'll have to admit the Boston show will always be special to me because I was holding a banner that said REAL MEN PLAY SOCCER and you motioned for me to come down front and you gave me a soccer ball. Thank You, from the bottom of "THIS OLD HEART OF MINE".

I have been a fan since "MAGGIE MAY" and this was the first time I had been to a final show of a tour and it was sad to think "IT'S ALL OVER NOW". "WHAT AM I GONNA DO". I thought "HOW LONG" before the next tour?

Rod, you have given so much of yourself to all your fans through the years and you have never let us down. Through the years, your music has helped me through some very difficult times, especially the last few because of my health. But you have taught me to "NEVER GIVE UP ON A DREAM". I have also enclosed a few pictures of my "Rod Room" and I am very proud of my collection and have always wanted you to see it.

HAPPY BIRTHDAY MY FRIEND !!

"YOU'RE IN MY HEART"

Rita Belcher

Steve & Kimberly

Dear Mr. Stewart.

I want to thank you from the deepest part of me heart for my many years of musical pleasure and for bringing my girlfriend Kimberly and I together. We are both members of your online fan club on America Online. I have been a fan for over 20 years and love each and every song (Except **Do You Think I'm Sexy**, smile, Rod!!!!) you have sung during your many years of performing. My favorite video is **Crazy About Her**. I have been to many of your concerts and you always amaze me with your energy and talent. As I write this, I get a tear in me eye, thinking back on all the emotions you have filled my heart with. All the years you have been with me, deep inside of me soul. All the trials and tribulations, bad times, sad times, you have been there for me through your magical voice. Thank you Rod!
Kimberly and I got to know each other somewhat like your video **This**. We met online and now are deeply in love. Thank God I found someone that I can share my love for you with. She was in line at the recent Coconuts signing for your **If We Fall In Love Tonight** release and you signed her copy of **Visual Documentary** written by John Gray. At our wedding, we will be sure to have your music playing when we are making our lifelong commitment to each other.

You will forever be in our hearts.

HAPPY BIRTHDAY ROD, DARLING OF THE MASSES, FOREVER

                        Love,

                        Steve and Kimberly

Peggy R

Fifty-two years ago on January 10th was born a little baby boy in north London. Little did his parents know he was destined to be loved by thousands of women, and more than a few men. He would grow up to be told by his mother, "Why don't you get a regular 9 to 5 job like your sister?" His father would say, "It's the biggest mistake I ever made." His brother Don would say, "He's the one with the money. I'm the one with the voice!"

So as we all know, a prophet is never appreciated in his own land, but not to worry, Roderick David, all of us crazy Rodnuts on the Rodnet love you forever and ever!

For example, I have driven 100 miles in a blizzard to see you (remember Philadelphia?), driven in another snow storm to Atlantic City, and am still paying 3-year auto insurance surcharges for an accident on the way to another concert.
It was all worth it, and I hope there will be many more concerts in the future to look forward to, even with such happenings.

Happy Birthday, Rod,

Peggy R

Happy Birthday Rod

The Smilers of the Rodnet

Graphics by Ty

Rod and Rachel Hunter.

Credits

There are so many people who contributed and helped with this book, and I just want to thank them. If I have missed anybody's name please forgive me, but you know who you are. Thanks for being such a great team!

The Smiler team; John Gray, Marilyn Kennedy and Rita Belcher. (Smiler is the best source for news and information on Rod Stewart). Juan Carlos Toledo Tomas, Rene Suiker, Frank Barrett, Patti Woolverton, Tracey Rasar, Sheila Gale, Shaun Tatarka, Ina Sassoon, The German Rod Stewart Fan Club: Storyteller, Rod Stewart Fanclub Deutschland, Schubertstrasse 1a, 44575 Castrop-Rauxel, Germany. Angela Jarvis, Debbie Fumagalli, Marcy Braunstein, Jo Wilhelm, Shannon Holliker, Cathy Deaton, Kathy & Gary Hurd, Sean Thomas, Janice Bernhard, Alan Jackson, Victor Rodriguez, Mike Gregor, Lynn Proctor, Thanks to Ty Turner for all his help. Thanks to Tracy for her Rod Stewart Survey.

Photo Credits

Collection of Ed Wincentsen: Page 10, 13.

Photos by Nancy Barr-Brandon:
Page 17, 56, 59, 60, 61, 81, 84, 85, 105, 114, 127, 140, 151, 167, 173.

Photos by Beth Carter: Page 24, 32, 33, 62, 63, 87, 106, 107, 141.

Photo by Cheryl Harrison: Page 30.

Photos by Lynn Proctor: Page 31, 53, 86, 90, 91, 92.

Photo by Cathy Deaton: Page 36.

Photos by Gary & Kathy Hurd: Page 39, 40.

Photos by Jo Wilhelm: Page 45, 46, 47, 54, 55.

Photo by Robin Whitmyer: Page 49.

Photos by Ed Wincentsen: Page 50, 51, 52, 100, 128, 129, 130, 131.

Photo by Alan Jackson: Page 83.

Photos by Marcy Braunstein: Page 110, 111.

Photos by Ty Turner: Page 118, 119.

Rod Stewart Photos Available for Sale

Nancy Barr-Brandon's photos of Rod Stewart are available for sale. See her photos that are listed on page 169.

For more information contact Nancy:

Nancy Barr-Brandon
P.O. Box B
Allenhurst, NJ 07711

Fax (732) 681-4501
email: catrescue@monmouth.com
phone: (800) 484-6455 (#3779)

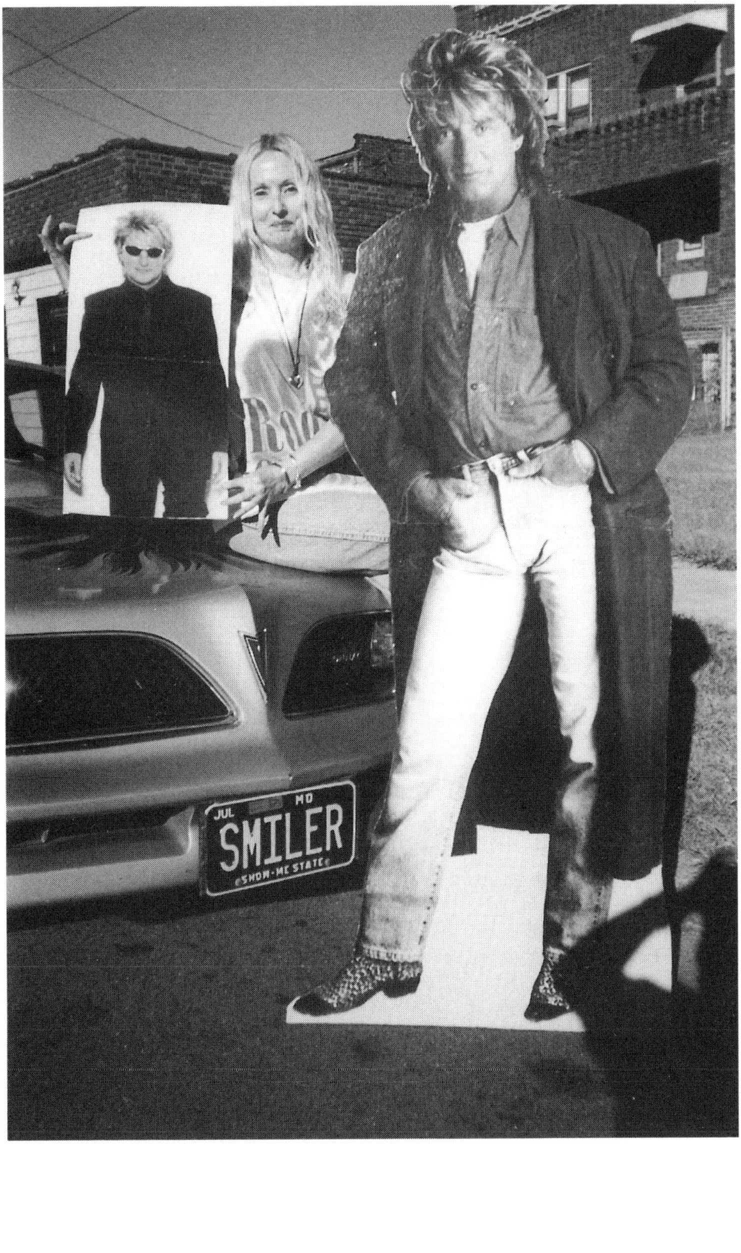
JUL
MO
SMILER
SHOW-ME STATE

SMILER
the official Rod Stewart Fan Club

P O Box 475
Morden
Surrey
SM4 6AT
England

The Rod Stewart Fan Club was founded in 1981 with Rod's personal support and full co-operation. The club is run for love of good music and not for profit. Smiler, the quarterly magazine is the basis and foundation of the club. It is a glossy, high quality, forty page publication containing color and black & white photos of Rod dating back to his childhood up until the present day. Smiler also contains features such as up to date news, interviews, special features and vintage press items. Smiler is now received in over 30 countries.

John Gray is the Fan Club President and Editor of Smiler. John was born in 1960 and bought his first Rod Stewart record in 1971. He first witnessed Rod live on stage in 1973 and since then has seen over 150 concerts worldwide.

Contact Information:

Smiler
P.O. Box 475
Morden, Surrey SM4 6AT, United Kingdom

Marilyn Kennedy, Smiler, UK Secretary
email: SmilerUK1@aol.com
Fax: 011-44-181-655-1505

Smiler USA
P.O. Box 796
Vinton, VA 24179

Rita Belcher, Smiler, North American Secretary
email: USSmiler@aol.com
Fax: 1-540-343-8771

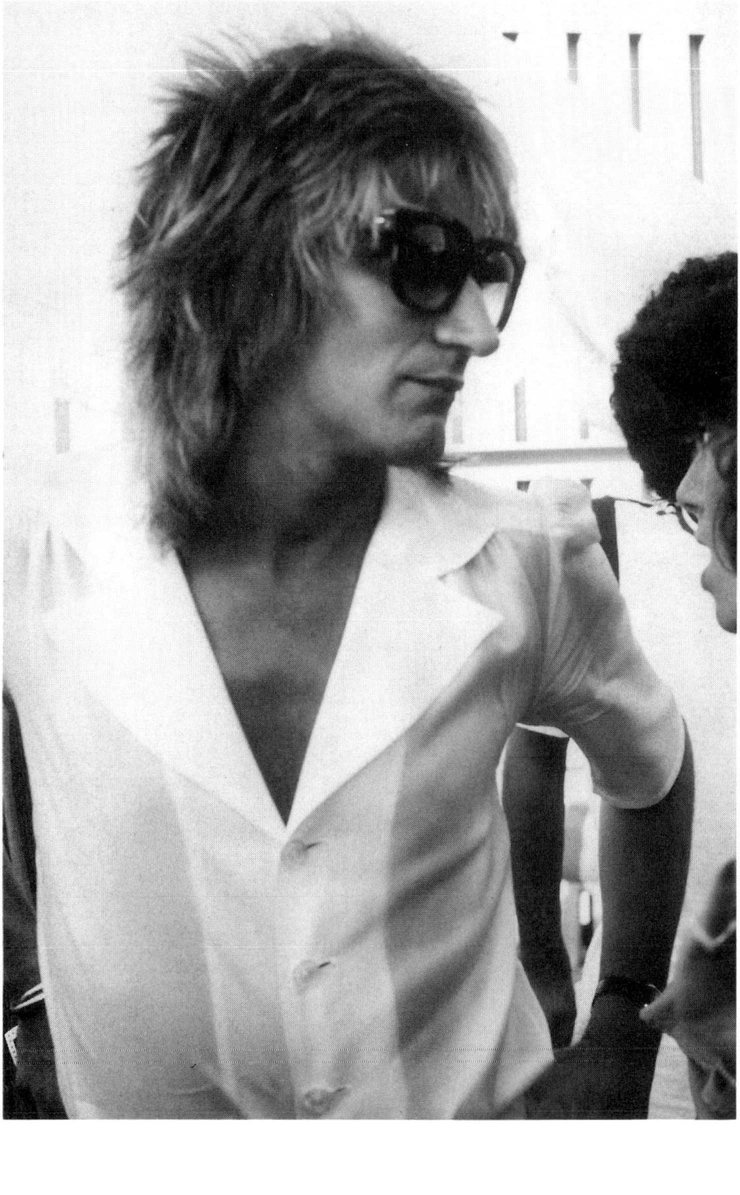